Writing Business Research Reports

A Guide to Scientific Writing

Matthew J. V. Rehart

Pyrczak Publishing
P. O. Box 39731
Los Angeles, CA 90039
(213) 660–7600

ISBN 0–9623744–6–6

Printed in the United States of America.

Contents

Notes:

Introduction

This book presents guidelines frequently followed by writers of reports of empirical research designed for publication in scientific business journals. The guidelines describe the types of information that should be included, how this information should be expressed, and where various types of information should be placed within a report. Excerpts from journal articles are used to illustrate most of the guidelines. At the end of each chapter, there are questions for classroom discussion.

Three groups of students should find this book useful. First, students whose professors require them to write research-based term papers that resemble journal articles should follow the guidelines. The exercises at the end of each chapter are designed for use by students in such classes. Second, graduate students who are writing theses and dissertations will find that almost all of the guidelines also apply to their writing. Interspersed throughout the text are pointers for such students. Students who are writing research proposals also will find that the guidelines apply to their writing.

What This Book Will *Not* Do for You

This book is not a traditional style manual that prescribes mechanical details such as how to cite references, the forms for levels of headings, typing requirements, and so forth. A number of excellent style manuals already do this; journals and universities often require their writers to follow the rules given in specific manuals. In addition, some journals provide guidelines on style and form, examples of which are provided in Appendices B through E.

Nor will you find here a discussion of the mechanics of standard English usage; it is assumed that you have already mastered these.

Finally, it is assumed that you have already selected a significant research topic, applied sound research methods, and analyzed the data. Thus, these topics are not covered.

Cautions in Using This Book

The guidelines suggested in this book are based on generalizations reached while reading extensively in business journals. If you are a student using this book in a research class, your professor may ask you to ignore or modify some of the guidelines you will find here. This may occur for two reasons. First, as a learning experience, your professor may require you to do certain things that go beyond the preparation of a paper for possible publication. For example, we suggest that the literature review for a journal article usually should be highly selective; your professor may wish to have you write a more extensive literature review in order to have you demonstrate your breadth of knowledge of the topic on which you have done empirical research. Second, as in all types of writing, there is a certain amount of subjectivity as to what constitutes effective writing; even experts differ. Fortunately, these differences are less pronounced in scientific writing than in many other types.

Experienced writers of research may violate many of the guidelines presented here and still write effective research reports that are publishable. Beginners are encouraged to follow the guidelines rather closely until they have mastered the art of scientific writing.

Using the Appendices

Appendix A provides a checklist of the guidelines described in this book. It should be used while writing and revising reports. While reviewing students' work, professors may wish to refer to the guideline numbers in their written comments on research reports (e.g., "See Guideline 5.2 in Appendix A").

Appendix B presents the Style Guide for Authors of journal articles, which is published once a year in the *Academy of Management Journal*.

Appendices C through E present general information for contributors from various journals. In these, you will find two types of information: (1) rules regarding mechanics such as the form for citing references and (2) guidelines for the effective expression of ideas in scientific reports; the vast majority of these guidelines are consistent with those that you will find in this book.

Appendix F is designed for evaluating journal articles. In most classes, it works best if an instructor assigns an article for all students to evaluate and then leads a classroom discussion of it.

Acknowledgments

I am grateful to Fred Pyrczak and Randall R. Bruce, who allowed me to borrow freely from their book, *Writing Empirical Research Reports: A Basic Guide for Students of the Social and Behavioral Sciences*, which provided the basic structure for this one.

Three anonymous reviewers provided helpful comments on the first draft of this manuscript. I am also indebted to Paula Cizmar, Kate Benson, and Jack Petit for their editorial assistance.

Matthew J. V. Rehart

$\mathscr{N}otes:$

Chapter 1

Writing Simple Research Hypotheses

In a single sentence, a simple research hypothesis describes the results that a researcher expects to find. In effect, it is a prediction. The following are guidelines for writing this type of hypothesis.

✔ Guideline 1.1

A simple research hypothesis should name two variables and indicate the type of relationship expected between them.

In Example 1.1.A, the variables are "level of verbal skills" and "ability to close a sale." They are called variables because subjects are expected to vary or differ on them (e.g., some subjects will have more highly developed verbal skills than others).

The hypothesis indicates that the researcher expects to find (1) higher levels of verbal skills among subjects who have greater ability to close a sale and (2) lower levels of verbal skills among subjects who have less ability to close a sale. (The hypothesis does *not* imply that the relationship is perfect. A "direct relationship" refers to an overall trend to which there may be many exceptions.)

Note that the word "positive" may be substituted for "direct" in Example 1.1.A without changing its meaning. "Direct" is usually preferred to "positive" in academic writing.

Example 1.1.A

> There is a direct relationship between level of verbal skills and ability to close a sale.

In Example 1.1.B, "retail price" is an independent or stimulus variable; its relationship to "sales volume" is stated in the hypothesis—in general, the lower the price, the higher the sales volume.

Note that the word "negatively" may be substituted for "inversely" in the hypothesis without changing its meaning. "Inversely" is usually preferred in academic writing.

Example 1.1.B

> The retail price of household cleaning products is inversely related to their sales volume.

Example 1.1.C also contains an independent variable—the frequency of performance evaluations. The anticipated relationship to improvement in job performance is clear in the hypothesis. This improvement is known as the outcome or dependent variable.

Example 1.1.C

Employees who are given quarterly performance evaluations will show greater improvement in job performance than those given annual performance evaluations.

In Example 1.1.D, two variables are named but the expected relationship between them is not stated. The Improved Version of Example 1.1.D makes it clear that the author believes that those with more free-floating anxiety have less ability to form friendships.

Example 1.1.D

Managers differ in their levels of free-floating anxiety, and they differ in their ability to form friendships with colleagues.

Improved Version of Example 1.1.D

There is an inverse relationship between managers' level of free-floating anxiety and ability to form friendships with colleagues.

✓ *Guideline 1.2*

When a relationship is expected only among a certain type of subject, the population should be mentioned in the hypothesis.

In Example 1.2.A, automobile salespeople are identified as the population of interest to the investigator, who believes that the relationship will be found in this population but may or may not be found in other populations.

Example 1.2.A

Among automobile salespeople, there is a direct relationship between level of verbal skills and ability to close a sale.

✔ ## Guideline 1.3

A simple hypothesis should be as specific as possible yet expressed in a single sentence.

In Example 1.3.A, the terms "computer literacy" and "computer use" are ambiguous. The Improved Version of Example 1.3.A is more specific—yet still stated in a single sentence.

Example 1.3.A

There is a direct relationship between administrators' computer literacy and computer use.

Improved Version of Example 1.3.A

Among administrators, there is a direct relationship between the amount of training they have had in the use of computers and the number of administrative tasks they voluntarily perform using computers.

A certain amount of subjectivity enters into the decision on how specific to make a hypothesis. It is usually not possible to replace all ambiguous terms with fully operational definitions (i.e., definitions that fully describe the physical attributes of a variable) in a hypothesis. These definitions should be provided elsewhere in a research paper. Guidelines for writing definitions are presented in Chapter 6.

In Example 1.3.B, "positive effectiveness" is vague. This flaw is partially corrected in the improved version.

Example 1.3.B

Administrators who provide wellness programs for their employees project positive effectiveness.

Improved Version of Example 1.3.B

Administrators who provide wellness programs for their employees receive higher employee ratings on selected leadership qualities than administrators who do not provide wellness programs.

The Improved Version of Example 1.3.B indicates that "effectiveness" will be defined in terms of employee perceptions. The "selected leadership qualities" and "wellness programs" will need to be more fully defined elsewhere in the research paper.

✓ *Guideline 1.4*

If a comparison is to be made, the elements to be compared should be stated.

Example 1.4.A

> Food products packaged in recycled containers will receive greater acceptance from young adult consumers.

In Example 1.4.A, it is not clear whether recycled containers are to be compared with new containers or whether young adult consumers' preferences for recycled containers are to be compared with those of other consumers. Either of the following improved versions is acceptable, depending on the researcher's purpose.

Improved Versions of Example 1.4.A

> Food products packaged in recycled containers will receive greater acceptance from young adult consumers than from older consumers.

OR

> Among young adult consumers, food products packaged in recycled containers will receive greater acceptance than those packaged in new containers.

Commonly used terms that begin comparisons that should be completed are *greater, less, more, fewer, higher,* and *lower*.

✓ *Guideline 1.5*

Because most hypotheses deal with the behavior of groups, plural forms should usually be used.

In Example 1.5.A, the terms *engineer's* and *his level* are singular. This problem has been corrected in the improved version by substituting the terms *engineers'* and *their level*.

Example 1.5.A

There is a direct relationship between an engineer's participation in administrative decision making and his level of job satisfaction.

Improved Version of Example 1.5.A

There is a direct relationship between engineers' participation in administrative decision making and their level of job satisfaction.

In the Improved Version of Example 1.5.A, the sex-role stereotype regarding engineers has been eliminated. It is important, of course, to avoid sex-role stereotyping throughout research papers.

✓ *Guideline 1.6*

A hypothesis should be free of terms and phrases that do not add to its meaning.

Example 1.6.A

Among secretaries, those who have been assigned to work on a modified shift of ten hours a day for four days per week will be found to have better attendance records than those secretaries who are assigned to a more traditional schedule of working eight hours a day for five days per week.

The Improved Version of Example 1.6.A is much shorter than the original version, yet its meaning is clear.

Improved Version of Example 1.6.A

Secretaries who work ten hours a day for four days per week will have better attendance than those who work eight hours a day for five days per week.

✓ *Guideline 1.7*

A hypothesis should indicate what will actually be studied—not the possible implications of the study or value judgments of the author.

Because the hypothesis in Example 1.7.A cannot be tested within a reasonable time frame, it probably is a statement of possible implications. The Improved Version of Example 1.7.A probably reflects more accurately the methodology that the author plans to use; it is also more specific. If the hypothesis is supported by data, the author may wish to speculate in the discussion section of the report on the implications of this finding for business when baby boomers reach retirement age. Guidelines for writing discussion sections are presented in Chapter 10.

Example 1.7.A

> The liberalization of Americans' attitudes on environmental issues affecting business will take a dramatic turn when baby boomers reach retirement age.

Improved Version of Example 1.7.A

> Baby boomers are more supportive of environmental legislation that has a negative impact on business than older citizens.

In Example 1.7.B, the author is expressing a value judgment rather than describing the anticipated relationship between the variables to be studied. The improved version more clearly indicates how "religion" will be treated as a variable and indicates the actual outcome, "incidence of employee theft of office supplies," that will be measured.

Example 1.7.B

> Religion is good for society.

Improved Version of Example 1.7.B

> Regular attendance at religious services is inversely associated with the incidence of employee theft of office supplies.

If the hypothesis is supported by data, the writer may wish to assert that less theft is "good" for society in the introduction to the research report or in the discussion section; such an assertion would be acceptable as long as it is clear from the context that the author recognizes the assertion as a value judgment and not as a data-based conclusion.

✓ Guideline 1.8

A hypothesis usually should name variables in the order in which they occur or will be measured.

Example 1.8.A

First-year job performance evaluations will have a direct relationship with scores on the ABC Employment Screening Examination.

Because employment examinations are normally taken prior to starting a job, reference to the examination should be made before reference to job performance evaluations, as in the Improved Version of Example 1.8.B.

Improved Version of Example 1.8.A

There is a positive relationship between scores on the ABC Employment Screening Examination and first-year job performance evaluations.

In Example 1.8.B, the natural order has been reversed because the type of feedback is a stimulus that is expected to influence the subsequent feelings of anxiety.

Example 1.8.B

> More free-floating anxiety will be observed among employees who are given inconsistent supervisory feedback than among those who are given consistent feedback.

Improved Version of Example 1.8.B

> Employees who are given consistent supervisory feedback will exhibit less free-floating anxiety than those who are given inconsistent feedback.

✓ *Guideline 1.9*

Avoid using the words "significant" or "significance" in a hypothesis.

These terms usually refer to the results of tests of statistical significance. Because most empirical studies include such tests, inclusion of the terms in a hypothesis is not necessary; sophisticated readers will assume that the results of significance tests will probably be reported in the results section of the research paper.

✔ *Guideline 1.10*

Avoid using the word "prove" in a hypothesis.

Empirical research relies on observations or measurements that are less than perfectly reliable; they usually involve only samples from a population; furthermore, there may be biases in procedures. For these reasons, errors are almost always present in the results of empirical studies. Thus, we cannot deduce a conclusive proof, as one might in mathematics, by using the empirical method.

✔ *Guideline 1.11*

Avoid using more than one term to refer to a given variable.

In Example 1.11.A, it is not clear whether the "objective-format questionnaire" is the multiple-choice format or some other objective format such as true-false. This problem is corrected in the Improved Version of Example 1.11.A.

Example 1.11.A

Consumers who are administered a multiple-choice product-satisfaction questionnaire and given token rewards for participating in the survey will be more likely to answer all questions than those who are administered the objective-format questionnaire without rewards.

Improved Version of Example 1.11.A

Consumers who are administered a multiple-choice product-satisfaction questionnaire and given token rewards for participating in the survey will be more likely to answer all questions than those who are administered the multiple-choice questionnaire without rewards.

Do not vary terms in an attempt to make your report more interesting; the purpose of a scientific report is to convey information accurately and clearly—not entertain.

Exercise for Chapter 1

The following questions are provided for review and classroom discussion. Because the application of many of the guidelines involves a certain amount of subjectivity, there may be some legitimate differences of opinion on the best answers to some of the questions.

Part A: Name the two variables in each of the following hypotheses.

1. Salespeople in retail clothing stores will initiate fewer conversations with overweight customers than with normal-weight customers.

2. Technical writers who are more skilled at building positive interpersonal relationships with their colleagues are perceived by their administrators as being more effective in communicating information than technical writers who are less skilled in building such relationships.

3. Among upper-level managers, authoritarianism and anxiety are directly related.

4. Children who are shown a commercial containing physical violence will demonstrate more aggressiveness during a free play period than children who are shown a control commercial that does not contain violence.

Part B: For each of the following hypotheses, name the guideline(s), if any, that were not applied. Revise each hypothesis that you think is faulty. In your revisions, you may need to make some assumptions about what the authors had in mind when writing the hypotheses.

5. The hypothesis is to prove that automotive products in boldly colored packages are more likely to be carefully examined by male consumers.

6. Employees differ in age and they also differ in their ability to attend to instructional presentations.

7. Among managers who are high achievers, there will be a higher level of rivalry with their colleagues.

8. Other things being equal, the greater the number of rewards, the better the performance.

9. There is a direct relationship between a secretary's score on the XZY Test of Manual Dexterity and her typing ability.

10. The economic agenda of the present administration is weak.

11. Among job applicants, there will be less test-taking anxiety among those who take a test-preparation course.

12. There will be a significant relationship between the number of times a product is advertised on television and its effectiveness.

13. Employees who take the new personal development course during released time from work will report greater self-insight than those who take the developmental workshop course after work.

14. Different subcultures view the business environment differently.

Part C: Write a simple hypothesis on a topic of interest to you. Include in the hypothesis a reference to a population. Then list the names of the two variables in your hypothesis.

Part D: Examine research reports in journals to locate a simple research hypothesis. Copy the hypothesis and bring it to class for discussion. Be prepared to identify the variables in the hypothesis and to evaluate it in light of the guidelines presented in this chapter.

Chapter 2

A Closer Look at Hypotheses

This chapter presents some advanced guidelines for writing hypotheses and explores some of the guidelines from Chapter 1 in more detail.

✔ Guideline 2.1

A "statement of the hypotheses" may contain more than one hypothesis. It is permissible to include them in a single sentence as long as the sentence is reasonably concise and its meaning is clear.

Example 2.1.A

> Waiters and waitresses who introduce themselves by name will receive larger tips and higher customer evaluations on overall service than those who do not introduce themselves.

In Example 2.1.A, there is one independent variable (introduction/no introduction) and two anticipated outcomes or dependent variables. Therefore, there are two hypotheses: (1) those who introduce themselves will receive larger tips, and (2) those who introduce themselves will receive higher customer evaluations than those who do not introduce themselves.

✓ *Guideline 2.2*

When a number of related hypotheses are to be stated, consider presenting them in a numbered or lettered list.

In Example 2.2.A, the authors present four numbered hypotheses. Note that they have organized them into two related sets.

Example 2.2.A[1]

> Four research hypotheses were developed from our consideration of the statistical and accounting graphics literatures. . . . Hypotheses 1 and 2 concern the use of graphs:
>
> *Hypothesis 1:* Graphs of key financial variables are more likely to be included in the annual reports of companies with 'good', rather

---

[1] Beattie & Jones (1992, p. 294)

than 'bad', performance in terms of earnings per share and profit before tax as profit indicators.

Hypothesis 2: Graphs of key financial variables are more likely to be included in the annual reports of companies with 'good', rather than 'bad', performance in terms of the variable graphed.

Hypotheses 3 and 4, developed with reference to the information manipulation literature, concern the effect and incidence of measurement distortion:

Hypothesis 3: Measurement distortion is likely to give a more, rather than less, favourable portrayal of the company's performance.

Hypothesis 4: Favourable measurement distortion is more likely to occur in the annual reports of companies with 'bad', rather than 'good', performance in terms of the variable graphed.

In Example 2.2.B, the authors have indicated the relationships among their hypotheses by using "a," "b," and "c" to indicate that three of the hypotheses are closely related.

Example 2.2.B [2]

Hypothesis 1: Protégés in informal mentorships will perceive that their mentors provide more psychosocial and career-related functions than protégés in formal mentorships.

Hypothesis 2a: Informal protégés will report higher levels of organizational socialization than formal protégés who will, in turn, report higher organizational socialization than nonmentored individuals.

Hypothesis 2b: Informal protégés will report higher levels of intrinsic job satisfaction than formal protégés who will, in turn, report higher intrinsic job satisfaction than nonmentored individuals.

---

[2] Chao, Walz, & Gardner (1992, p. 621–623)

Hypothesis 2c: Informal protégés will have higher salaries than formal protégés who will, in turn, have higher salaries than nonmentored individuals.

Hypothesis 3: There will be a positive relationship between mentorship functions (psychosocial and career related) and job outcomes (organizational socialization, job satisfaction, and salary) for both formal and informal protégés.

✓ *Guideline 2.3*

The hypothesis or hypotheses should be placed before the section on methods.

The method section describes how the researcher tested the hypothesis. Therefore, the hypothesis should be stated before describing the methods used.

Hypotheses are usually stated in the paragraph(s) immediately preceding the major heading of "method." Occasionally, they have their own subheading, which is more common in theses and dissertations than in journal articles.

✓ *Guideline 2.4*

It is permissible, but *not* recommended, to use terms other than *hypothesis* to refer to a hypothesis.

The context provided by the article and placement of the statement just before the method section usually make it clear that a hypothesis is being stated even if it is referred to as an *expected result*, *speculation*, or other term. Such variations are shown in Examples 2.4.A and 2.4.B. They do not bother seasoned readers of research. For term projects, theses, and dissertations, students should usually use the term *hypothesis*.

Note that in Example 2.4.A, the hypotheses are preceded by the subheading *expected results*. Because they are predictions of the outcomes of the study, they are clearly hypotheses.

Example 2.4.A[3]

Expected Results

If feedback is used as a device to estimate what the organization will do, then expectations of advancement will be based on feedback from the organization's hierarchy. . . . However, if expectations of advancement are based on perception of the quality of performance, then feedback from the task will have a stronger relationship with expectations of advancement. A corollary is that self-evaluation would be as good a predictor of expected advancement as was feedback.

Example 2.4.B[4]

On the basis of the above evidence, it was speculated that gaze and touch (on the arm), along with the appropriate selection of interviewer sex . . ., would lead to greater compliance with a request to participate in a shopping mall interview concerning questions on advertising and television viewing behavior.

---

[3]Greller (1992, p. 1324)
[4]Hornik & Ellis (1988, p. 540)

✓ *Guideline 2.5*

A hypothesis may be stated without indicating the type of relationship expected between variables, but to qualify as a hypothesis, it must specify that some unknown type of relationship is expected.

Such a hypothesis is known as a "nondirectional" hypothesis because it does not specify the direction of the relationship.

Example 2.5.A is nondirectional because it does not indicate which group of managers are predicted to be more authoritarian; it does, however, indicate that there will be a difference (i.e., socio-economic background is associated with authoritarianism).

Example 2.5.A

Managers who were reared in low socioeconomic status families will differ in their level of authoritarianism from managers who were reared in middle socioeconomic status families.

Example 2.5.B also illustrates a nondirectional hypothesis; it only says that there will be a difference; it does not specify the direction of the difference.

Example 2.5.B

Males and females will differ in their preferences for advertising scenarios in which a recognized expert makes a recommendation on consumer products.

Nondirectional hypotheses are less frequently used in research than directional hypotheses. This is probably true for two reasons: (1) researchers often have opinions about the variables they study, and their opinions often lead them to formulate directional hypotheses, and (2) when researchers do not wish to speculate on the direction of a relationship, they may substitute a statement of the research purpose or research question for a hypothesis. This type of substitution is discussed in detail in Chapter 3.

✔ *Guideline 2.6*

When a researcher has a research hypothesis, it should be stated in the research paper; the null hypothesis does not always need to be stated.

A research hypothesis is the hypothesis that the researcher believes will be supported by his or her data. For most research hypotheses, there are no direct statistical tests of the significance of the differences or relationships postulated. Rather, significance tests are designed to test null hypotheses, which state that there is no true relationship or difference in the population from which the samples were drawn.

Whenever a significance test is conducted, it is understood by the sophisticated reader that a null hypothesis is being tested. Thus, in most academic journals, formal statements of null hypotheses are omitted.

In term projects, theses, and dissertations, students are often required to state the null hypothesis in order to demonstrate that they understand what is being tested statistically. Examples 2.6.A and 2.6.B illustrate some ways in which the null hypothesis can be stated. Because there is more than one way to state a null hypothesis, two statements of the null hypothesis are shown in each example. Only one statement, of course, would be included in a research paper.

Example 2.6.A

Research Hypothesis: Private school graduates have a higher proportion of fathers in high-status occupations than public school graduates.

Corresponding Null Hypothesis: There is no difference in the proportion of fathers in high-status occupations between the populations of private school and public school graduates.

Another Version of the Null Hypothesis: The observed differences between the proportions of fathers in high-status occupations for private school graduates and public school graduates are the result of chance variations associated with the random sampling process.

Example 2.6.B

Research Hypothesis: Social standing in informal organizational networks is directly related to gregariousness.

Corresponding Null Hypothesis: There is no true relationship between social standing in informal organizational networks and gregariousness.

Another Version of the Null Hypothesis: The relationship between social standing in informal organizational networks and gregariousness is nonexistent in the population from which the sample was drawn.

✔ *Guideline 2.7*

Avoid using the word "significant" in the statement of the null hypothesis.

The word "significant" refers to a test of statistical significance that will be used to determine whether a null hypothesis should or should not be rejected. Because all null hypotheses should be tested with tests of significance, it is superfluous to incorporate a reference to significance testing into a statement of the null hypothesis.

In the Improved Version of Example 2.7.A, the word "true" has been substituted for the word "significant." A statistician defines a "true difference" as the difference that would be found if the variables could be studied without the presence of sampling errors (i.e., chance or random errors).

Example 2.7.A

There is no significant difference in comprehension of annual reports between those shareholders who first read a 500-word summary and those who do not read the summary.

Improved Version of Example 2.7.

There is no true difference in comprehension of annual reports between those shareholders who first read a 500-word summary and those who do not read the summary.

Exercise for Chapter 2

In this exercise, you are asked to examine examples of published research in journals as well as theses and dissertations. There is no better way to learn the conventions followed in writing reports of empirical research than extensive reading of such reports.

1. Review journal articles and locate a statement that contains two or more hypotheses incorporated into a single sentence. Copy the statement and bring it to class for discussion.

2. Review journal articles and locate a statement that consists of a numbered list of three or more hypotheses. Copy the list and bring it to class for discussion.

3. Review three journal articles that contain explicit statements of hypotheses and make note of the following:
   a. In how many cases are the hypotheses stated in the last paragraph (or last few paragraphs) before the "method" sections?
   b. In how many cases are the hypotheses stated in the last sentence before the "method" sections?
   c. In how many cases did the authors use alternative terms such as *expected results* or *speculate* rather than *hypotheses* to identify the hypotheses?
   d. How many of the hypotheses were directional and how many were nondirectional? If both types are found, copy an example of each.

4. Examine theses or dissertations in your college/university library. Copy a research hypothesis and the corresponding null hypothesis and bring it to class for discussion.

5. Write a set of related directional research hypotheses on a topic of interest to you. For each research hypothesis, write a corresponding null hypothesis.

6. Rewrite one of the hypotheses that you wrote for item number five to make it a nondirectional hypothesis.

Notes:

Chapter 3

Writing Research Purposes, Objectives, and Questions

Sometimes researchers do not state hypotheses either because they are not interested in examining relationships between variables or because they believe that there is too little knowledge on a topic to permit formulation of hypotheses. Under these circumstances, a research purpose[1] or research question should be substituted for a hypothesis. In addition, sometimes a general statement of the research purpose(s) precedes a statement of specific hypotheses.

The following guidelines indicate when to state research purposes or questions, and they illustrate the application of some of the guidelines in Chapters 1 and 2 when writing them.

---

[1] Sometimes a research purpose is called a research objective.

✓ *Guideline 3.1*

When there are many hypotheses, consider providing a general statement of purpose before stating the specific hypotheses.

A general statement of the research purpose provides readers with an overview that helps them anticipate the types of hypotheses that will be stated and understand why they were examined together in a single study.

In Example 3.1.A, the statement of the general purpose (called an *objective* in this case) was provided by the author in the first paragraph of his research article.[2] It provides an overview of the topic that is covered by the literature review (which immediately follows in the article) and sets the stage for the hypotheses, which are shown in Example 3.1.B.

Example 3.1.A[3]

> The objective of the research reported in this paper is to examine the perceptions and attitudes of different user-groups to the role of the budget, budget pressure and budget participation.

Example 3.1.B[4]

> Hypothesis 1: the three user-groups will have a similar view of the budget as primarily a forecast of future performance rather than as a motivational target.
>
> Hypothesis 2: the three user-groups will each believe that the major role of the budget in their company is as a control device.

---

[2] Note that a general statement of purpose may, instead, be placed after the literature review but before the hypotheses.
[3] Lyne (1992, p. 357)
[4] Lyne (1992, p. 358)

Hypothesis 3a: the three user-groups will agree that the use of the budget as a control device will produce pressure on employees.

Hypothesis 3b: the user-groups will have different attitudes towards the existence of dysfunctional behaviour caused by budget pressure; in particular, accountants will experience less pressure and consequently display less resentment and less dysfunctional behaviour.

Notice that hypotheses 3a and 3b in Example 3.1.B both deal with pressure and, thus, have the same identifying number.

✔ *Guideline 3.2*

When the goal of research is to describe variables without describing relationships among them, state a research purpose or question instead of a hypothesis.

Example 3.2.A

The purpose of our research project was to collect empirical data on what the traditional graduate training programs in marketing were doing to provide formal didactic and practical training on ethical issues in advertising.

A hypothesis would not be an appropriate substitute for Example 3.2.A if the authors plan only to report percentages on each of the separate questions in their survey without relating them to each other (e.g., reporting how many programs provide formal training without relating it to other variables such as institution size).

Notice that the purpose in Example 3.2.A could have been stated as a research question, as illustrated in Example 3.2.B.

Example 3.2.B

> What are the traditional graduate training programs in marketing doing to provide formal didactic and practical training on ethical issues in advertising?

The choice between stating a research purpose or a research question is a matter of choosing the form that reads more smoothly in a particular context. One form is not inherently preferable to the other.

✔ *Guideline 3.3*

Research purposes or questions should be stated when not enough is known to permit formulation of hypotheses.

Because much of the research in journals, theses, and dissertations is theory-driven, hypotheses are usually stated. Occasionally, however, there is insufficient information to tie a problem to a specific theory or there are competing theories that an author wishes to explore. Example 3.3.A, which was stated in the introduction to a journal article, illustrates the latter situation.

Example 3.3.A [5]

    The purpose of this paper is to develop an integrated approach, combining concepts from expectancy theory, goal-setting theory, and individual characteristics research, to examine factors that affect the performance of software development professionals.

    Example 3.3.B shows a research objective (i.e., purpose), which was stated immediately before the heading of *method*, which is the place hypotheses are often stated.

Example 3.3.B [6]

    Our objective in this research was to investigate the relationship between individual-differences, job/job-characteristics, context, and environmental factors and the facility with which a new job is learned. We analyzed the incremental relationships beyond that associated with time on the job. Our primary emphasis was on job/job characteristics and context factors, while individual-differences and environmental factors received secondary and tertiary attention, respectively.

✓ *Guideline 3.4*

A research purpose or question should be as specific as possible, yet stated concisely.

---

[5] Rasch & Tosi (1992, p. 396)
[6] Morrison & Brantner (1992, p. 929)

The need for specificity in hypotheses is discussed in Chapters 1 and 2. Application of this guideline to hypotheses, purposes, and questions is often more difficult than one might realize at first. Consider, for instance, Example 3.4.A shown below. It is quite specific, actually naming a specific instrument (i.e., measuring tool). However, for a reader who is not familiar with the Areas of Change Questionnaire, the research purpose may be too specific. Thus, a writer must judge whether his or her audience is likely to be familiar with the specific item(s) mentioned—in this case, the specific questionnaire.

Example 3.4.A

> The purpose was to determine whether managers in the military are more likely to endorse certain items on the Areas of Change Questionnaire than their civilian counterparts and to determine whether item endorsement varies as a function of sex.

For readers who are not familiar with the Areas of Change Questionnaire, the Improved Version of Example 3.4.A is superior, even though it does not name the specific questionnaire; notice, however, that the improved version is more specific as to what the items measure.

Improved Version of Example 3.4.A

> The purpose was to determine whether managers in the military are more likely to endorse questionnaire items relating to change in the face of uncertainty than their civilian counterparts and to determine whether item endorsement varies as a function of sex.

✓ *Guideline 3.5*

When a number of related purposes or questions are to be stated, the author should consider presenting them in a numbered or lettered list.

Example 3.5.A[7]

> 1. Does a salesperson's . . . [communication style (CS)] exert a significant influence on sales performance?
>
> 2. Which dimensions of CS have the most influence on sales outcome?
>
> 3. Does the influence of one dimension of CS depend upon the value of the other CS dimensions? Is there an interaction effect between CS dimensions?

The numbered list in Example 3.5.A allows the author to refer to individual hypotheses by number later in the report; this possibility is discussed in Chapter 9.

Exercise for Chapter 3

1. Briefly describe two conditions under which it would be better to state a research purpose or question rather than a research hypothesis.

---

[7]Dion & Notarantonio (1992, p. 64)

2. In general, should the research question format be preferred over the research purpose format?

3. Review journal articles and locate a statement that consists of a numbered list of purposes or questions. Copy the list and bring it to class for discussion.

4. Review three journal articles that contain explicit statements of purposes or questions and make note of the following:
   a. In how many cases are the purposes and questions presented shortly before the section on methods?
   b. In how many cases are the purposes and questions stated in the last paragraph before the section on methods?
   c. In how many cases has the author made it clear in the introduction why purposes or questions were stated instead of hypotheses?

5. Write a research purpose on a topic of interest to you. Then, rewrite it in order to make it into a research question. Which form (i.e., purpose or question) do you prefer? Why?

Chapter 4

Writing Titles

The following are guidelines for writing titles for empirical research reports.

✔ Guideline 4.1

If only a small number of variables are studied, the title should name the variables.

In Example 4.1.A, the variables are (1) placement of advertisements and (2) message persuasiveness.

Example 4.1.A

The Relationship Between Placement of Advertisements in News Magazines and Message Persuasiveness

Notice that the title in Example 4.1.A is not a complete sentence and does not end with a period mark; these are appropriate characteristics of titles.

✓ *Guideline 4.2*

If many variables are studied, only the types of variables should be named.

For example, a researcher might examine how consumers' attitudes toward discount warehouses change over time with attention to differences among urban, suburban, and rural groups; various socioeconomic groups; the sexes; and so on. Because there are too many variables to name in a concise title, only the major variable(s) need to be named. In Example 4.2.A, the major variable is "change in attitudes toward discount warehouses"; the other variables, which are not specifically named, are referred to as "demographic variables."

Example 4.2.A

> Changes in Consumers' Attitudes Toward Discount Warehouses and Their Relationships with Selected Demographic Variables

✓ *Guideline 4.3*

The title of a journal article should be concise; the title of a thesis or dissertation may be longer.

Titles of journal articles tend to be concise. A simple survey illustrates this point. A count of the number of words in the titles of a random sample of journal articles in recent issues of the *Journal of Marketing Research*, the *Journal of Management Studies,* and the *Journal of Retailing* revealed that the median (average) number of words was only 10. Example 4.3.A is the shortest and Example 4.3.B is the longest.

Example 4.3.A[1]

Corporate Rejuvenation

Example 4.3.A is exceptionally short and might be improved by incorporating the names of the variables associated with corporate rejuvenation that were studied.

Example 4.3.B[2]

Measuring the Short-Term Effect of In-Store Promotion and Retail Advertising on Brand Sales: A Factorial Experiment

Example 4.3.B clearly indicates the types of variables studied and the method of study. If the authors wished to make it closer in length to the average, they might consider deleting the words "measuring" and "factorial."

---

[1] Stopford & Baden-Fuller (1990, p. 399)
[2] Bemmaor & Mouchoux (1991, p. 202)

Example 4.3.C shows a title of about average length for the sample of titles examined.

Example 4.3.C [3]

Determining Interbrand Substitutability Through Survey Measurement of Consumer Preference Structures

A random sample of titles of dissertations on marketing and management in recent issues of *Dissertation Abstracts International* revealed that the median number of words in the titles was 15, considerably more than the median of 10 for journal articles. The longest dissertation title in the sample is shown in Example 4.3.D.

Example 4.3.D [4]

The Effects of a Decision Support System on Novice Personnel Managers in their Evaluation of Candidates Applying for Programmer/Analyst Positions

Theses and dissertations are, in fact, tests; they permit students to demonstrate the breadth of their knowledge as well as their ability to write precise, detailed descriptions—which may account for the average difference in title length between journals and dissertations.

---

[3] Bucklin & Srinivasan (1991, p. 58)
[4] Chang (1991, p. 214A)

✓ Guideline 4.4

A title should indicate what was studied—not the results of the study.

All of the previous examples illustrate this guideline. Example 4.4.A violates the guideline; it is corrected in the improved version.

Example 4.4.A

Introducing a New Product at a Lower Price than the Regular Price Adversely Affects Subsequent Sales at the Regular Price

Improved Version of Example 4.4.A

The Effects of Introducing a New Product at a Lower Price than the Regular Price on Subsequent Sales at the Regular Price

Guideline 4.4 may surprise some beginning students of empirical methods because outcomes and conclusions are often stated in titles in the popular press. This is the case because, quite often, the press reports straightforward facts; "Five Die in Downtown Hotel Fire" is a perfectly acceptable title for a factual article of limited scope. Because research articles in academic journals are likely to raise as many questions as they resolve, a title that states a simple factual conclusion is usually inappropriate.

✓ *Guideline 4.5*

Mention the population(s) in a title when the type(s) of population(s) are important.

Example 4.5.A[5]

> The Transaction Costs Theory of Joint Ventures: An Empirical Study of Japanese Subsidiaries in the United States

By indicating that Japanese subsidiaries in the United States are the population, the authors have indicated an important element of the study.

✓ *Guideline 4.6*

Consider the use of subtitles to indicate the methods of study or amplify the variable(s) mentioned in the main title.

In Examples 4.6.A and 4.6.B, the subtitles indicate the types or methods of study, while the main titles name the variables. This arrangement is helpful to readers who are scanning tables of contents for articles of interest to them; usually the variables are of primary interest while the method of study is secondary.

---

[5] Hennart (1991, p. 483)

Example 4.6.A[6]

Consumer Price and Promotion Expectations: An Experimental Study

Example 4.6.B[7]

Impression of Retail Stores: A Content Analysis of Consumer Images

In Example 4.6.C, the authors use the subtitle to amplify the primary variable named in the main title.

Example 4.6.C[8]

Safety of Children in Grocery Stores: The Impact of Carseat Use in Shopping Carts and Parental Monitoring

It is usually *inappropriate* to name the primary variables in a subtitle. In Example 4.6.D, the main title names the populations, which, while important, are probably less so than the names of the variables examined.

Example 4.6.D

Marketing to Consumers: The Relationship Between Camera Angle and the Perception of Sexual Embeds in Underwear Advertisements

---

[6] Kalwani & Yim (1992, p. 90)
[7] Zimmer & Golden (1988, p. 265)
[8] Harrell and Reid (1990, p. 531)

Note that the term "marketing to consumers" is probably not needed, especially if the article is published in a marketing journal.

✓ Guideline 4.7

A title may be stated in the form of a question; this form should be used sparingly and with caution.

Example 4.7.A is cast in a form that implies that the answer will be a simple "yes" or "no," which is seldom the case in empirical research. This problem has been corrected in the improved version.

Example 4.7.A

Does Video Feedback Improve the Communication Skills of Sales Managers?

Improved Version of Example 4.7.A

To What Extent Does Video Feedback Improve the Communication Skills of Sales Managers?

Titles in the form of questions may suggest that straightforward answers will be found in the research article. Because this is often not the case in empirical research reports, such titles should be used sparingly and with caution because they may be misleading.

Questions, when used as titles, have a less formal feel than titles in the form of statements. Thus, the question form sometimes may be preferred in less formal types of publications such as staff newsletters and workshop materials.

✓ Guideline 4.8

Use the words *effect* and *influence* in titles with caution.

The words *effect* and *influence* are frequently used in titles of research in which cause-and-effect relationships are examined. To examine such relationships, true experimental, quasi-experimental, or rigorous ex post facto methods should be employed; as a general rule, only the titles of reports employing these methods should contain these words.

Examples 4.8.A and 4.8.B illustrate the typical use of the word *effects* in a title; the general form is "The effects of an independent variable (treatments) on a dependent variable (outcomes)."

Example 4.8.A[9]

Effects of Repeating Varied Ad Executions on Brand Name Memory

Example 4.8.B[10]

Effects of Training on Behaviors of the Selection Interview

---

[9]Unnava & Burnkrant (1991, p. 406)

[10]Gatewood, Lahiff, Deter, & Hargrove (1989, p. 17)

Effects is used as a noun in Examples 4.8.A and 4.8.B. As a noun, it means *influence*. The word *affect*, when used as a noun, means *feelings* or *emotions*. Clearly, *effect* is the correct noun to use in these examples.

It is *not* necessary to incorporate the word *experiment* into a title containing the word *effects* (e.g., references to the experimental method should be deleted in these examples: "An Experimental Study of the Effects of X on Y" or "The Effects of X on Y: An Experimental Study") because the word *effects* is closely associated with experimental research. It is widely known that the purpose of an experiment is to investigate the effects (or influence) of one or more independent variable(s) on one or more dependent variable(s).

✓ *Guideline 4.9*

A title should be consistent with the research hypothesis, purpose, or question.

In Example 4.9.A, two research hypotheses are stated; the corresponding title reflects the content of the hypotheses. In this example, the authors state their expectations in the hypotheses but, properly, not in the title.

Example 4.9.A[11]

> *Hypotheses:*
>
> 1. Effective and ineffective interviewers will use different decision strategies. Specifically, there will be differences in the relative weighting of cues as a function of interviewer effectiveness.
>
> 2. Effective interviewers will be more aware of their decision processes than ineffective interviewers.
>
> *Corresponding Title:*
> Interviewer Decision Processes and Effectiveness: An Experimental Policy-Capturing Investigation

In Example 4.9.B, the title clearly parallels the research purpose.

Example 4.9.B[12]

> *Research Purpose:*
>
> The purpose of the study was to explore advertisers', agencies', and media/regulatory organizations' perceptions of comparative advertising on a number of important dimensions.
>
> *Corresponding Title:*
> Comparative Advertising: Views from Advertisers, Agencies, Media, and Policy Makers

---

[11] Graves & Karren (1992, p. 313)
[12] Muehling, Stem, & Raven, (1989, p. 38)

✓ *Guideline 4.10*

Avoid clever titles, especially if they fail to communicate important information about the report.

Example 4.10.A

Publishing in the 1990s: Things Gutenburg Never Taught You

Only one word in Example 4.10.A is informative: "publishing." The reader will assume that an article deals with contemporary issues unless the title indicates that the study is historical. Note that the subtitle states what is *not* covered—it should indicate what *is* presented.

In general, throughout a research paper, avoid the temptation to be clever. Usually, it distracts serious readers and reduces the effectiveness of the communication.

✓ *Guideline 4.11*

Use brand names in titles sparingly.

This guideline is suggested because most investigators are interested in investigating relationships that may hold true over a variety of specific brands. For practical reasons, they may examine only a limited number of brands in their study but wish to discuss the results in terms of a theory that might generalize across a larger number of brands; mentioning a brand name in a title suggests that the results are brand-specific.

The authors of the title in Example 4.11.A applied Guideline 4.11 when writing their title even though they examined only Gillette, Edge, and Calvin Klein advertisements in their study.

Example 4.11.A[13]

> The VASE Scales: Measures of Viewpoints About Sexual Embeds in Advertising

Exercise for Chapter 4

Part A: Comment on the adequacy of each of the following titles for research articles.

1. Personnel Psychologists Have More Positive Attitudes Toward Statistics as a Tool for Understanding Human Behavior than Managers

2. The Correlates of Salesperson Performance at Toyota and Nissan Dealerships

3. Managerial Performance

4. Background Music in Television Advertising

---

[13] Widing, Hoverstad, Coulter, & Brown (1991, p. 3)

5. The Effects of Sentence Length on Comprehension of Magazine Advertisements: An Experiment Conducted in Five Major Urban Areas from 1993 Through 1995 Using Samples that Vary in Terms of Highest Level of Education Completed, Age, Socioeconomic Status, and Race

6. Are Age and Tenure Related to Job Satisfaction?

7. Forbidden Fruit Tastes Especially Sweet: A Study of Executives' Ethical Behavior

8. The Effects of Individual and Group Counseling Employing Cognitive, Behavioral, Interpersonal, and Humanistic Counseling Techniques on Situational Stress Among Employees at IBM

Part B: Select two of the hypotheses, purposes, or questions presented in Chapters 1, 2, or 3 and write an appropriate title for each.

Part C: Name a purpose for research on a topic of interest to you and write an appropriate title.

Chapter 5

Writing Introductions and Literature Reviews

The purpose of an introduction in an empirical research report is to introduce a problem area, establish its significance, and indicate the author's perspectives on the problem. It usually concludes with a statement of the research hypotheses, purposes, or questions to be answered by the study.

In journal articles, the introductory material is usually integrated with the literature review into a single essay. Most institutions of higher education require that the introduction and the review of literature in a thesis or dissertation be presented in separate chapters.

The guidelines that follow apply to all types of empirical research reports and proposals except where noted.

✓ *Guideline 5.1*

Consider starting the introduction by describing the problem area and gradually shift its focus to specific research hypotheses, purposes, or questions.

To implement Guideline 5.1, first write a topic outline of what will be covered. Example 5.1.A shows a simple outline that illustrates Guideline 5.1. Such an outline should be prepared early in the writing process and then revised and made more detailed as the writer obtains more literature on the topic.

Example 5.1.A

Topic Outline for Introduction
1. Importance of question-asking by employees
    a. As a functional skill to solicit job-related information
    b. As a social skill used in interactions with other employees
2. Introduction to two types of questions
    a. Requests for factual information (Who, What, and When)
    b. Questions about causation (Why)
    c. Functions of the two types in business communications
3. Relationship between supervisors' verbal behavior and employees' verbal behavior
    a. On other verbal variables such as acceptance of criticism
    b. On question-asking behavior: quantity and type
4. Relationship between culture and verbal behavior
    a. Examples of how and why cultures may vary
    b. Functions of questions in target cultures
5. Statement of research purposes

    a. Determine types and numbers of questions asked
      by employees in specific employment settings

    b. Determine relationship between question-asking
      by supervisors and by employees, with attention to both
      number and type

    c. Determine relationship between question-asking
      and cultural background in target cultures, with attention
      to minority cultures that are underrepresented in the settings

If the above outline were for an introduction in a thesis or dissertation, the author would write the introduction with emphasis on his or her own views and observations regarding these topics with few citations to published literature; reference to the fact that certain topics will be covered in more detail in the literature review, which is usually the second chapter, would be appropriate.

If Example 5.1.A were an outline for an introduction to a journal article, the literature review would be integrated with the author's introductory remarks.

✓ Guideline 5.2

In long introductions and literature reviews, consider the use of subheadings to guide readers.

The numbered topics in Example 5.1.A (e.g., *Importance of question-asking by employees, Introduction to two types of questions*) could be used as subheadings.

In theses and dissertations, where the introduction and the literature review are usually each a fairly long chapter, the use of subheadings is especially desirable. Begin each chapter with an overview of what is covered in it, and begin each subsection with such an overview. This is illustrated in Example 5.2.A, in which the first paragraph provides an overview of the chapter, and the second paragraph provides an overview of the first subsection.

Example 5.2.A

CHAPTER 2
LITERATURE REVIEW

This chapter describes literature relevant to the research purposes of this thesis. It is organized into four sections: (1) the importance of question-asking by employees, (2) introduction to two types of questions, (3) relationship between supervisors' verbal behavior and employees' verbal behavior, and (4) relationship between culture and verbal behavior. At the end of each section, the relevance of the literature to the research reported in this thesis is discussed.

Importance of Question-Asking by Employees

Most of the literature on the importance of question-asking deals with the behavior of students in school settings. This literature is briefly reviewed first in order to establish the importance of question-asking while learning; interspersed are commentaries on possible implications of this research for question-asking in business settings. Then, the more limited literature on question-asking as a functional skill to solicit job-related information and as a social skill used in interactions with other employees is reviewed in detail. Throughout, there is an emphasis on the principles of learning theory and theories of social interaction that underlie the literature reviewed.

Doe (1993), in a major survey of question-asking in adult vocational schools, found that. . . .

✓ *Guideline 5.3*

The significance of a topic should be explicitly stated in the introduction to a term paper, thesis, or dissertation.

Colleges and universities sometimes require that the introduction to a thesis or dissertation contains a subsection on the significance of the research topic. Be specific in giving reasons for the importance of a topic, as illustrated in Example 5.3.A.

Example 5.3.A

Investigation of the training needs of employment counselors who work with individuals who are HIV+ is important because the number of individuals with HIV continues to increase, creating greater demand for counselors trained in this area; AIDS tends to occur more frequently in certain minority groups, which may have unique psychological needs and which are often underrepresented in higher-level positions; and information on HIV and its treatment continues to emerge at a rapid rate, creating the need for ongoing training of employment counselors.

Long, detailed statements of the significance of research topics are less common, although usually acceptable, in journal articles.

Authors of articles often assume that their readers are specialists who already understand the importance of their topics and, thus, often provide less detailed descriptions of significance than are typically found in theses and dissertations. It is always a good idea, though, to indicate in the introduction why the original research being reported is significant to the field as was done in Example 5.3.B, which is the first sentence in the second paragraph of the introduction in a journal article on how consumers' motivational and emotional states relate to patronage. The authors are clearly establishing the importance of studying patronage.

Example 5.3.B [1]

> It is arguable that the ultimate survival of all retail establishments depends on providing outlet features that generate patronage among . . . consumers.

Example 5.3.C is the first paragraph in an article in which the authors examine the role of retail price advertisements in shaping store-price image. This paragraph not only introduces the problem area (see Guideline 5.1) but also establishes its importance.

Example 5.3.C [2]

> Over the years, price has continued to be one of the most important bases upon which retailers compete. As originally noted by McNair (1958), many innovative retail institutions have entered the market emphasizing a low price appeal (e.g., department stores in the mid-19th century, supermarkets in the 1930s, and discount stores in the 1950s). When these institutions have subsequently de-

---

[1] Dawson, Bloch, & Ridgway (1990, p. 408)
[2] Cox and Cox (1990, p. 428)

emphasized price in order to provide various consumer amenities, they in turn have become vulnerable to newer breeds of price-oriented competitors.

✓ Guideline 5.4

A statement of significance should be specific to the topic investigated.

Example 5.4.A

Human resource is one of the greatest resources of this country, and education plays a major role in maintaining, nurturing, and protecting that resource. It is imperative that we find, evaluate, and utilize systems that yield the results that are necessary for the country's progress.

Example 5.4.A was submitted as the statement of significance in the first draft of the proposal for a thesis in which an employment skills program in adult schools was to be evaluated. Notice that the statement fails to deal specifically with employment skills in adult education. In fact, the statement is so broad, it could refer to almost any curriculum and instruction topic.

✓ Guideline 5.5

Use of the first person is acceptable; it should be used when it facilitates the smooth flow of the introduction, but it should be used sparingly.

Use of the first person is especially appropriate when referring to the author's personal observations, experiences, and beliefs, as is the case in Example 5.5.A.

Example 5.5.A

> This problem began to intrigue me when I directed a major marketing campaign to which consumer reponse was quite lukewarm.

The use of *I* in Example 5.5.A is less stilted than the use of *this author*. Frequent use of the first person throughout the introduction and elsewhere in the research report, however, shifts the focus away from the content of the report, as in Example 5.5.B

Example 5.5.B

> When I realized that all the previous research on this topic was descriptive, I decided that I would undertake an experimental study.

Improved Version of Example 5.5.B

> Because all the previous research on this topic was descriptive, an experimental study seemed to be in order.

Although the use of the first person is more frequently used in contemporary reports than it was in the past, its use is still relatively rare. Thus, beginning students should avoid using the first person if they have any doubts about its appropriateness in a particular context.

✓ *Guideline 5.6*

The literature review should be presented in the form of an essay—not in the form of an annotated list.

An annotation is a brief summary of contents; a list of annotations indicates what research is available on a topic but fails to organize the material for the reader because it does not indicate how the individual citations relate to each other and what trends the author has observed in the research.

An effective review of the literature is an essay organized around a topic outline (see Guideline 5.1) and takes the reader from topic to topic. The literature on a topic is cited during the discussion of that topic. Articles with similar findings or methodologies may be cited together, as in Example 5.6.A, in which the author interwove a number of references into a single, coherent paragraph. Notice that some of the authors are cited at more than one point in the paragraph; the paragraph clearly is organized around the points the author wishes to make about what the literature says and *not* organized around specific references.

Example 5.6.A[3]

> Numerous disciplines provide theoretical and empirical support for the efficacy of reward schemes that pay for performance. Social psychologists using experimental methods have found that performance-based pay serves to enhance effort and upgrade workforce quality (Landau and Leventhal, 1976; Leventhal, 1976). Economic theorists have also argued that performance-contingent rewards motivate effort and attract talent when effort and talent are not easily observed (Holmstrom, 1979; Levinthal, 1988). Organization scholars have cited similar benefits of distributing rewards based on performance (Lawler, 1981; Milkovich and Wigdor, 1991). Consistent with achieving these objectives, the majority of organizations claim to use some form of performance-based pay, particularly for exempt employees (Peck, 1984; Milkovich and Wigdor, 1991).

Note that in the Harvard method for citing references, only the authors' last names and year of publication are given. The names may be made part of the sentence, as in Example 5.6.B, or they may be included parenthetically at the end of the sentence, as in Example 5.6.C. In 5.6.B, the emphasis is on the authorship; in 5.6.C the emphasis is on the content or idea being expressed. The choice among forms hinges on the emphasis you wish to make; including the names parenthetically is usually preferred in academic reports of research; the main exception is when the writer wishes to emphasize that the point was made by a well-known authority.

---

[3]Zenger (1992, p. 198)

Example 5.6.B

> Doe (1994) found that a major source of dissatisfaction among secretaries is the low social status accorded to their occupation both within business organizations and in society in general.

Example 5.6.C

> A major source of dissatisfaction among secretaries is the low social status accorded to their profession both within business organizations and in society in general (Doe, 1994).

✔ *Guideline 5.7*

The literature review should emphasize the findings of previous research—not just the methodologies and variables studied.

Example 5.7.A

> The role of management consultants as agents of both radical strategic changes and changes in the way executives think about their environment have been examined (Ginsberg & Abrahmanson, 1991).

Example 5.7.A violates the guideline; in the improved version, the major finding is summarized.

Improved Version of Example 5.7.A

Results of a recent study suggest that management consultants are more effective in stimulating changes in the way executives think about their environment than in stimulating radical strategic changes (Ginsberg & Abrahamson, 1991).

✓ *Guideline 5.8*

Point out trends and themes in the literature.

This guideline was followed by the authors of Example 5.8.A, which is the first paragraph of their article.

Example 5.8.A[4]

Although much socialization research and theory has given primary emphasis to the adopting of normative attitudes, values, goals, and culture of the organization (e.g., Schein, 1968; 1988 ; Van Maanen, 1976; Van Maanen & Schein, 1979), more recent perspectives have addressed the learning process that occurs as newcomers assimilate to the organization. In these newer perspectives, the organizational level issues are more distal to newcomers, whereas content areas closer to the individual, such as tasks and roles, are recognized as important for adjustment. For example. . .

Note the use of *e.g.* (meaning *for example*) in Example 5.8.A. This indicates to the reader that these are only selected references for the point being made; use of *e.g.*, which does not need to be

---

[4] Ostroff and Kozlowski (1992, pp. 849–850)

italicized, is desirable in journal articles if there are many references for a specific point. In a thesis or dissertation, a student's committee may wish to have a more comprehensive list of citations presented in the text, indicating that the student was thorough in his or her search of the literature.

✓ *Guideline 5.9*

Point out gaps in the literature.

In Example 5.9.A, gaps in the literature are noted by the author.

Example 5.9.A[5]

> . . . despite voluminous anecdotal and survey research indicating that women in organizational settings lack access to or are excluded from emergent interaction networks (e.g., Kanter, 1977; Harlan and Weiss, 1982; Ragins and Sudstro, 1989; O'Leary and Ickovics, 1992), little empirical research has investigated the role of networks in creating or reinforcing gender inequalities. Because the differential allocation of network rewards may partially account for gender differences . . . the role of sex differences in informal networks warrants further investigation.

Because the author of Example 5.9.A is introducing a study on sex differences in network structure, pointing out the gap helps to

---

[5] Ibarra (1992, p. 422)

establish the need for her study. Using the literature review to establish the need for a study is covered by the next guideline.

Students who are writing term papers, theses, and dissertations should be aware that when they point out gaps in the literature, they may be asked by their professors and committee members to defend such an assertion. Thus, it is a good idea to keep careful records of how the literature search was conducted (i.e., what indices and data bases were examined—including the dates) and which descriptors (i.e., subject index terms) were used in the search. Students should consider including a statement such as the one in Example 5.9.B in their reports; such statements are usually *not* included in journal articles.

Example 5.9.B

A search of the ABC Index for the years 1950 through 1994 using the subject index terms of "term a" and "term b" yielded only two surveys (i.e., Doe, 1988; Jones, 1990) and no experimental studies on this topic.

✓ Guideline 5.10

Use the literature review to establish the need for the current study.

The author of Example 5.10.A cites statements by others that more research is needed on a given topic.

Example 5.10.A [6]

Managers are constantly required to listen; yet, researchers know less about listening than speaking, reading, or writing. Further research is needed to establish the exact nature of the listening process and provide direction for those seeking to improve individuals' listening competence in organizational settings (Hunt & Cusella, 1983; Mundale, 1980; Raudsepp, 1980).

The author of Example 5.10.B concludes her literature review with the paragraph shown in Example 5.10.B.. She is using the literature review, as a whole, to establish the importance of her topic of study.

Example 5.10.B [7]

All of the above literature suggests that British women, and women in general, are still responsible for the care and development of their children. There is still a pervading assumption that a woman should fit her job/career around the child(ren) and that, although the male partner will help out, it is nevertheless the woman's role. Hence, her job/career will suffer. Most writers, recognizing this, have bemoaned the fact, declaring it to be an "injustice." The present study was undertaken to look at what women themselves think about this "double burden," especially in terms of the attitudes of working mothers toward their domestic responsiblites.

---

[6] Brownell (1990, p. 402)
[7] Newell (1992, p. 39)

✓ *Guideline 5.11*

The author should feel free to express opinions about the quality and importance of the research being cited.

The authors of Example 5.11.A criticize several studies for using small samples.

Example 5.11.A[8]

> Existing idiographic studies (Dougherty et al., 1986; Kinicki et al., 1990; Valenzi & Andrews, 1973; Zedeck et al., 1983) of interviewers in single organizations used relatively small samples (3 to 10 interviewers) that did not allow full exploration of individual differences across interviewers. Thus, the issue of whether there are large within-firm differences in the interviewers' decision processes needs further exploration.

If no statement is made about the special strengths and weaknesses of previous research being cited, a reader is likely to assume that the author of the literature review believes that the research methodology was reasonably sound. Thus, it is not necessary to comment on the adequacy of all the research cited.

Note that pointing out weaknesses in the literature is an effective way to justify a new study in which these weaknesses will be overcome.

---

[8] Graves and Karren (1992, p. 317)

✓ Guideline 5.12

The literature review for a journal article should be highly selective; the review for a thesis or dissertation may be less selective.

The main criteria for selection should be relevance to the topic and the quality of research. Recency of publication usually should be a minor criterion in the selection of literature (see Guideline 5.13). In a thesis or dissertation, however, the student may wish to demonstrate his or her knowledge of recent literature by citing all of it regardless of quality, while pointing out major weaknesses. In a journal article, citations of research that is only peripheral to the topic or very methodologically weak may be omitted.

✓ Guideline 5.13

Consider citing older literature in order to provide a historical context for the present study.

Following Guideline 5.13 is especially desirable in a thesis or dissertation if the writer wishes to demonstrate a comprehensive knowledge of the literature on a topic; it is also appropriate in journal articles when the writer wishes to acknowledge the original proponent of a theory or principle that underlies the current study. This was done in Examples 5.13.A and 5.13.B.

Example 5.13.A[9]

The routinization of administrative work and the regularization of tasks were central tenets of Weber's (1946) bureaucratic archetype. Weber was one of the first to underscore the importance of bureaucratic routine as an antidote to the caprices of autocratic rules. Early leaders in the scientific management movement also. . .

Example 5.13.B[10]

Berle and Means' (1932) original managerialist theory of corporate control maintained that the ownership of large corporations is dispersed; therefore, the influence of owners on the action of managers is limited. Monitoring of the actions of top managers. . .

✓ *Guideline 5.14*

Use direct quotations sparingly in literature reviews.

This guideline holds for three reasons. First, direct quotations often do not convey their full meaning without context; quoting the context is usually less efficient than paraphrasing the main idea(s) of the author. Second, frequent quotations may disrupt the flow of the review because of the varying styles of the authors. Finally, quotations often bog the reader down in details that are not essential for the purpose of providing an overview of literature.

Direct quotations are appropriate when the writer of the review (1) wants to illustrate either the original author's skill at

---

[9] Bozeman, Reed, & Scott (1992, p. 291)
[10] Boeker (1992, p. 403)

writing or lack thereof and (2) believes that the wording of a statement will have an emotional impact on the reader that would be lost in a paraphrase. These purposes seldom arise in presenting literature in an empirical research report.

✓ Guideline 5.15

Report sparingly the details of the literature being cited.

When the research being cited has already been published, the reader may obtain copies to learn the details. Thus, it is not necessary to summarize extensively the details of such literature.

Typically, reviews of literature in theses and dissertations contain more details on cited research than reviews of literature in journal articles. Even in theses and dissertations, however, the author should be selective in reporting details.

When commenting on the quality of research being cited (see Guideline 5.11), brief reference should be made to those characteristics that make it strong or weak. Detailed descriptions of weaknesses usually are needed only if the author's own study was designed to overcome those specific weaknesses.

Concluding Comments

For many students, writing the introduction and review of literature is the most difficult part of writing an empirical research report. The guidelines presented above will only help you avoid some of the major pitfalls; they do not cover the other important matters in effective writing such as providing clear transitions and writing with a sparse but clear style. The latter can be mastered only through guided learning under the tutelage of an experienced writer and through extensive reading of effective prose.

If you lack confidence in your ability to write introductions and literature reviews, follow these rules:

1. Write a topic outline as illustrated under Guideline 5.1 and take it with you when you consult with your instructor or committee. The outline will help them understand what you are trying to accomplish and make it easier for them to help you.

2. Read numerous reviews of literature, paying attention to how they are organized and how the authors make transitions from one topic to another.

3. After writing a first draft, first have it reviewed by friends and colleagues—even if they are not experts on your topic. Ask them to point out elements that are not clear. Effective introductions are usually comprehensible to any intelligent layperson.

4. Be prepared to revise and rewrite. Because effective writing is achieved through this process, expect that your instructor, committee, or journal editor will request revisions.

Exercise for Chapter 5

1. Examine the introductions to three journal articles on a topic of interest to you and answer the following questions.

a. How many are organized according to Guideline 5.1? How many follow some other organizational pattern? Explain.

b. In how many does the author explicitly state why the research topic is significant? If any, copy one statement and bring it to class for discussion.

c. In how many does the author use the first person? If any, copy an example and bring it to class for discussion.

d. In how many is the literature review integrated with the introduction?

e. In how many does the author express opinions on the quality of at least some of the literature cited? If any, copy an example and bring it to class for discussion.

f. In how many are one or more direct quotations included? If any, copy an example and be prepared to discuss whether you think that its inclusion is appropriate.

g. To what extent are details of previous research cited?

2. Examine the introductions and reviews of literature in four theses or dissertations. Answer questions a through g in question 1.

3. Write a topic outline for an introduction to a research project of interest to you. Have it reviewed by two friends or colleagues and revise it in light of their comments. Bring to class both the first and second drafts for discussion.

Notes:

Chapter 6

Writing Definitions

Two types of definitions are usually found in empirical research reports. Conceptual definitions, which broadly define important terms, are often presented in the introduction. Operational definitions, which define traits and procedures in concrete, step-by-step physical terms, are usually presented in the section on methods.

In theses and dissertations, conceptual definitions are sometimes presented in a separate section of the introduction with its own subheading. In journal articles, conceptual definitions are usually integrated into the introductory statement. Often, authors of journal articles assume that their readers are familiar with the general concepts and, thus, do not provide formal statements of conceptual definitions. In both types of reports, operational definitions should be provided in the section on methods.

This chapter presents guidelines on what to define and how to write conceptual and operational definitions.

✔ *Guideline 6.1*

All of the variables in a research hypothesis, purpose, or question should be defined.

Example 6.1.A shows a hypothesis (identified as H1, meaning the first hypothesis in a series). "Advertising scenario of competition with others" and "advertising scenario of self-competition" are defined by describing the advertisements used in the study.

Example 6.1.A[1]

H1: Males would prefer an advertising scenario of competition with others to an advertising scenario of self-competition.

Ad 1—Competition with others is depicted from four males playing racquetball in a court. TING is shown on the sidelines. (Slogan: "After a Day of Rigorous Competition Against Others, Reach for TING.")

Ad 2—Competition with self is depicted from a single male playing in a racquetball court. (Slogan: "When Competing Against Myself, All I Need is TING.")

In Example 6.1.B, the second sentence provides an informal definition of the "intention-behavior link" mentioned in the objective.

---

[1]Prakash (1992, p. 46)

Example 6.1.B [2]

> Our second objective is to examine whether certain factors (primarily demographic and product-usage-related) moderate the intention-behavior link. That is, what kinds of respondents saying they will "definitely" (or "immediately") purchase will indeed buy?

In Example 6.1.C, a definition of "discount advertised" is provided parenthetically.

Example 6.1.C [3]

> As the discount advertised (AD, defined in this study as the percentage off regular price) by retailers increases, consumers' perceptions of the discounts or savings are also likely to increase.

✓ *Guideline 6.2*

Most abbreviations should be defined the first time they are used.

Abbreviations that you use frequently and, thus, seem very familiar to you may not be known by all of your readers. Thus, it is important to define all but the most universally used abbreviations (e.g., certain abbreviations for units of measurement are so widely used that they do not need to be spelled out.)

It is essential to define abbreviations invented for use in a particular research paper, as was done in Examples 6.1.C above and

---

[2] Morwitz & Schmittlein (1992, p. 393)
[3] Gupta & Cooper (1992, p. 402)

6.2.A below. Notice that in Example 6.2.A, the author refers to specific types of behaviors to help define the traits, which is desirable.

Example 6.2.A[4]

> These have been defined by Hall, as borrowing from two extreme behaviors, which he calls Monochronism (M time) and polychronism (P time). Individuals working under M time do one thing at a time and tend to adhere to preset schedules. P time, on the contrary, stresses involvement of people who do several things at the same moment, easily modify preset schedules, and seldom experience time as "wasted."

In Example 6.2.A, the author cites definitions offered by another person. This is perfectly acceptable.

✓ *Guideline 6.3*

Theories and models on which a thesis or dissertation are based should be formally defined. In a journal article, the author may choose to provide an informal definition and refer the reader to a publication in which it is described in detail if the theory is well-known in the author's field.

Example 6.3.A

> In the introduction to a thesis, a student states, "The results will be discussed against the background of the deprivation model."

[4]Usunier (1991, pp. 199–200)

The "deprivation model" mentioned in Example 6.3.A should be defined.

✓ *Guideline 6.4*

Conceptual definitions should be specific.

The authors of Example 6.4.A provide brief, but relatively specific, conceptual definitions of three variables. Bracketed numbers were added to help you identify them.

Example 6.4.A [5]

> Kahn et al. defined [1] work conflict as the extent to which a person experiences incompatible pressures within the work domain and [2] family conflict as the extent to which a person experiences incompatible pressures within the family domain. [3] Work-family conflict, as defined by Kahn, is a form of interrole conflict in which the role pressures from the work and family domains are mutually incompatible in some respect. That is, participation in the work (family) role is made more difficult by virtue of participation in the family (work) role.

The authors of Example 6.4.A chose to cite a definition previously offered by an expert. This is perfectly acceptable.

---

[5] Higgins, Duxbury, & Irving (1992, p. 53)

✓ *Guideline 6.5*

Operational definitions should be provided. As noted above, these are usually stated in the method section of a report or proposal.

An operational definition is a definition in terms of physical steps. After reading an operational definition, the reader should be able to see in his or her mind's eye the physical operations that were used to measure a variable, to give treatments, to define a population, or to identify the relevant aspects of a model or theory.

Example 6.5.A

Creative fluency was defined as the ability to produce many creative solutions to a problem within a standard time frame.

Example 6.5.A is not operational because one cannot picture the exact problem—what was and what was not judged as creative—and the length of the standard time frame. The improved version is more operational.

Improved Version of Example 6.5.A

Creative fluency was defined as the number of uses a subject could name for a one-foot ruler during one minute.

Example 6.5.B is not operational because the reader does not know what specific physical things were done in the presence of the subjects. This has been corrected in the improved version.

Example 6.5.B

The stress-producing condition used for the experimental group was a mild verbal threat given by the experimenter.

Improved Version of Example 6.5.B

In order to produce the stress-producing condition for the experimental group, the subjects were seated by an experimenter who was dressed in a white doctor's jacket. The experimenter introduced himself as a physician and stated that for the purposes of the experiment, "Prior to your interview for the position, you will be given a physical exam. As part of the exam, we will administer a mild electric shock to you while we measure your blood pressure."

✓ *Guideline 6.6*

If a published instrument was used, the variable measured by that instrument may be operationally defined by citing the reference for it.

Example 6.6.A

In this study, verbal intelligence is defined as performance on the Verbal Scale of the Wechsler Adult Intelligence Scale: Revised (Wechsler, 1981).

Because most published tests cannot be reproduced legally and because many are too long to reproduce in a research report, reference to a test, as in Example 6.6.A, is sometimes the only way to provide an operational definition.

The Wechsler Adult Intelligence Scale: Revised is a popular test of intelligence, and most readers interested in this topic are likely to be familiar with it. For published tests that are not well known, writers should provide an overview of their physical characteristics (e.g., types of items, number of items, and time limits) and their statistical properties, especially reliability and validity data.

✓ *Guideline 6.7*

If an unpublished instrument was used, the whole instrument should be reproduced in the report or a source for a copy of the instrument should be provided in order to define operationally the variable that was measured.

If a very short instrument, such as a short questionnaire, is used, a copy may be included in the body of the report. Longer instruments should be included in an appendix in a thesis or dissertation. Authors of journal articles should be prepared to supply copies of longer unpublished instruments to readers who request them. Providing sample test items in a journal article, when this will not violate test security, is a good way to increase the operationalization of variables measured with longer instruments.

Guideline 6.7 was followed by the authors of Example 6.7.A who defined "union instrumentality" by providing the actual wording of the items and stating that the items were rated on three-point Likert scales; Likert scales are the widely used scales that usually have four or five points that range from "strongly agree" to "strongly disagree."

Example 6.7.A[6]

> **Union instrumentality.** Three items measured union instrumentality: (1) "Unions make sure that employees are treated fairly by supervisors," (2) "Unions help working men and women to get better wages and hours," and (3) "Unions interfere with good relations between companies and employees" (reverse scored).

The operational definition in Example 6.7.A was placed in the method section of the report; writing method sections is discussed in more detail in Chapter 8.

✓ *Guideline 6.8*

Operational definitions should be sufficiently specific so that another investigator can replicate a study with confidence that he or she is examining the same variables under the same circumstances.

A replication is an attempt to reproduce the results of a study by using the same methods. Replicability is the major criterion for judging the reliability of the results of empirical research. Inability to replicate results casts serious doubts on the validity of earlier studies.

---

[6] Davy & Shipper (1993, p. 191)

Even definitions that appear to be highly operational at first glance may be inadequate when one attempts to replicate a study. The definition in Example 6.8.A illustrates this point. As one prepares to replicate a study involving this variable, questions about the physical process quickly arise: How large were the letters? What type of equipment was used to flash the letters? What type of screen was used? What type of film was used to produce the letters? and so on. Answers to these questions could easily affect the subjects' ability to recognize letters of the alphabet.

Example 6.8.A

> Visual acuity was defined as the ability to name letters of the alphabet when flashed on a screen in a random order for a period of two seconds for each letter.

Guideline 6.8 often is not followed to the letter. In practice, the writer must consider how operational a definition needs to be in order to permit a reasonably close replication. For making fine discriminations among very similar shapes, answers to the questions posed about Example 6.8.A may be crucial to a successful replication.

✓ *Guideline 6.9*

Even a highly operational definition may not be a useful definition.

An operational definition that is too narrow or is too far afield from how others define a variable may be inadequate. Example

6.9.A illustrates this point. It is fairly operational, but the definition of "self-concept" is much more narrow than that used by most psychologists.

Example 6.9.A

> Self-concept was defined as the number of times each job applicant smiled during the first 15 minutes of an employment interview. A smile was defined as a noticeable upward turn where the lips meet—based on agreement by three independent observers. Each observer was an experienced employment counselor. Counts of smiles were made from videotapes, which permitted the observers to reexamine facial expressions that were questionable.

Concluding Comments

Writing satisfactory operational definitions is often much more difficult than it might appear at first. When writing them, assume that you are telling someone exactly how to conduct your study. Then have your definitions reviewed by colleagues and ask them if they could perform the same study in the same way without requesting additional information. Use their comments in revising your definitions.

Exercise for Chapter 6

Part A: For each of the following definitions, describe what additional types of information are needed, if any, to make it more operational.

1. Anxiety was defined as manifest signs of anxiety during an employment interview.

2. Hispanic customers were defined as those customers whose surnames appeared on a master list of Hispanic surnames developed by the author in consultation with two linguistic experts. This list may be obtained by writing to the author at P.O. Box xxx, Any City, State, Zip Code.

3. In this study, stress was defined as the condition that resulted from telling employees that their success on a task that they were about to undertake would be used to make decisions about their advancement in the organization.

4. Sales performance was defined as number of sales completed.

5. Job satisfaction was defined as agreement with this statement: "If I had it to do over again, I would accept employment in my current job."

Part B: Examine three research articles in journals and note how the variables in the research hypotheses, purposes, or questions are defined. Copy the definition that you think is most operational and bring it to class for discussion.

Part C: Follow the directions for Part B but examine three theses or dissertations.

Part D: For each of the following variables, write a highly operational definition. Because you may not have studied some of these variables, do not concern yourself with whether your definitions are highly useful (see Guidelines 6.8 and 6.9).

6. ability to accept criticism from superiors

7. effectiveness of a television commercial

8. attitudes toward chemical companies

9. respect for authority

10. an innovative method of presenting an advertisement in a weekly news magazine.

Part E: Name a variable that you might wish to study. Write a conceptual definition of it and then write a highly operational definition. Try to make your operational definition both very operational and very useful (see Guidelines 6.8 and 6.9). For this activity, do not cite a published test or scale in order to define the variable you have selected. Have the definitions reviewed by colleagues and revise them. Bring both drafts of the two definitions to class for discussion.

Chapter 7

Writing Assumptions and Limitations

An assumption is a statement that the author believes is true even though the direct evidence of its truth is either absent or very limited.

A limitation is either (1) a weakness or handicap that potentially limits the validity of the results or (2) a boundary to which the study was knowingly confined. The latter is sometimes called a "delimitation" in a thesis or dissertation. For example, if a researcher wanted to study general creativity among advertising executives but used only a measure of creative drawing, this would be a limitation in the first sense because it is a weakness in the execution of the study; if the researcher only wanted to study creative drawing and deliberately chose a measure of only this aspect of creativity, his or her findings would be delimited to this type of creativity, which is not a flaw in light of the investigator's purpose.

Explicit statements of assumptions, limitations, and delimitations often are required in theses and dissertations; these provide students with an opportunity to demonstrate that they understand the potential weaknesses in their research. Such statements are often included in Chapter 1, each with its own subheading. With the permission of their instructors, students may, instead, integrate the statements throughout their papers (e.g., discuss limitations of sampling when they describe the sampling procedure in the chapter on methods) or include such statements in the discussion chapter, which is usually the last chapter. (Writing discussions is described in detail in Chapter 10.)

Authors of journal articles integrate statements about assumptions and limitations in various sections of their articles, including the introduction, method section, and discussion section; limitations are frequently discussed in the discussion section, which is usually the last section. These authors usually are very selective in deciding which assumptions and limitations to state, naming only the ones that may seriously affect the outcomes of their studies.

✓ *Guideline 7.1*

In the statement of an assumption, consider stating the reason(s) why it was necessary to make the assumption.

In Example 7.1.A, Guideline 7.1 has been violated because it states what was assumed but not why the assumption was necessary. Because no measure of human behavior is perfectly valid, Example 7.1.A adds little to the report. In the improved version, the author describes the circumstances that led to the use of a scale that may be of limited validity.

Example 7.1.A

It was assumed that the authoritarianism scale was valid.

Improved Version of Example 7.1.A

Because it was not possible to make direct observations and ratings of authoritarianism over time in a variety of managerial settings, a self-report measure was administered. Therefore, it was necessary to assume that the subjects were honest in reporting their typical behaviors associated with authoritarianism.

✔ *Guideline 7.2*

If there is a reason for believing an assumption is true, state the reason.

If the sentence in Example 7.2.A were added to the Improved Version of Example 7.1.A, a basis for making the assumption would be indicated.

Example 7.2.A

To encourage honest responses, the questionnaires were administered anonymously and the subjects were encouraged to be open and honest by the assistant who administered the scale.

The last sentence in Example 7.2.B also describes the basis for an assumption.

Example 7.2.B

> Because the investigator could not be present during all of the sessions while the experimental method was being used, it was necessary to assume that the managers consistently and conscientiously used the method. This assumption seems tenable because the managers were given intensive training, as described in the procedures section, and reported enthusiasm for the method, as described in the results section.

✓ *Guideline 7.3*

If an assumption is highly questionable, consider casting it as a limitation.

If the author has no basis for making the assumption in Example 7.3.A, the circumstance should be treated as a limitation—as was done in the Improved Version of Example 7.3.A.

Example 7.3.A

> A certain number of the potential subjects refused to participate (15 of the 38 contacted by the male interviewer). . . . It was assumed that the nonrespondents were similar to the respondents in their rate of . . . failures.

Improved Version of Example 7.3.A[1]

> A certain number of the potential subjects refused to participate (15 of the 38 contacted by the male interviewer), either not responding on the telephone, or refusing to come in for an interview. Therefore, the sample actually studied necessarily excluded the uncooperative participants. It might reasonably be guessed that the subjects who refused to participate would have distorted their reports even more than those who cooperated because they likely contained a higher proportion of . . . failures.

The author of the Improved Version of Example 7.3.A refers to the circumstance as a "methodological problem," indicating that it is a limitation in the first sense described at the beginning of this chapter.

✓ *Guideline 7.4*

Consider speculating on the possible effects of a limitation on the results of the study.

The author followed this guideline in the last sentence of the Improved Version of Example 7.3.A. The last sentence in Example 7.4.A also illustrates this guideline; the authors speculate on the results that might have been obtained with a larger sample. Note that small sample size is frequently a limitation in empirical research.

---

[1] Reider (1987, pp. 35–36)

Example 7.4.A[2]

> Given a larger sample of subjects, we would likely find that soup is a product category where consumption intentions are best estimated through volume measures while consumption intentions for cranberry sauce would be best estimated through likelihood measures.

✓ *Guideline 7.5*

When space permits, be specific in a statement of limitations.

Example 7.5.A shows a statement of limitations in a study on peer reporting of unethical behavior. Notice that the first sentence, while covering an important point, would *not* be, by itself, sufficiently specific to the study being reported. Additional sentences in the article (only some of which are shown in the example) indicate how this limitation applies to the particular study being reported.

Example 7.5.A[3]

> In the scenario studies, the methodology and the range of contexts limit the generalizability of the results. Although the subjects seemed to have placed themselves in role, they were not in a real situation with real consequences like ostracism from the group. In any scenario study, the level of subject involvement in the situation is limited. However, this limited involvement should operate to

---

[2] Wansink & Ray (1992, p. 14)
[3] Trevino & Victor (1992, p. 58)

reduce the subjects' responsiveness to the manipulation, suggesting that significant study results may be considered more robust. Further, the academic cheating scenario is closely related to these subjects' current experience, and the subjects for the fast-food theft scenario study had an average of more than a year of relevant work experience.

Concluding Comments

Authors of journal articles include information about limitations for an important reason—to warn readers about weaknesses that may affect the interpretation of the results. Students who write term papers, theses, and dissertations have an additional reason for including them—to demonstrate to their instructors that they understand the limitations of their research. Students who have written explicit, detailed statements of limitations will be in a better position to defend their work before a thesis or dissertation committee.

Exercise for Chapter 7

1. Examine three theses or dissertations that contain explicit statements of assumptions. (The section on assumptions, if any, will often be listed in the table of contents.) How many assumptions were written in accordance with both Guidelines 7.1 and 7.2? If any, copy one and bring it to class for discussion. If none, copy

an assumption and name the guideline(s) that were not followed.

2. How many of the individual assumptions that you examined for question 1 involved generalizing from a sample to a population? How many involved the measuring tools or tests? How many involved the administration of experimental treatments? How many involved other issues? Name them.

3. Examine three journal articles that contain explicit statements of limitations. In how many did the authors speculate on the possible effects of the limitations on the results of their studies? (Note: This type of speculation may appear in the final, i.e., discussion, section.) If any, copy an example and bring it to class for discussion.

4. How many of the individual limitations that you examined for question 3 involved generalizing from a sample to a population? How many involved the measuring tools or tests? How many involved the administration of experimental treatments? How many involved some other issue?

5. How many of the individual limitations that you examined for question 3 describe weaknesses and how many describe boundaries to which the study was deliberately confined? (Note: The authors may refer to both types as simply *limitations*.) If both types are included, copy an example of each.

6. Suppose you mailed a questionnaire to each member of a population but only 28 percent completed the questionnaires and returned them to you. Suppose that you have no information on how the nonrespondents differ from the respondents. Would you describe this circumstance as an assumption or as a limitation? Why?

7. Suppose you used a scale that had been validated for the type of population that you were studying. Suppose that the scale had high validity but, as with all tests, was less than perfectly valid. Would you describe this circumstance as an assumption or as a limitation? Why?

8. Suppose you conducted an experiment with an experimental and control group and you took extreme care to be sure that both groups were treated in the same way (e.g., same lighting, temperature, seating arrangement, etc.) except for the administration of the experimental treatments to the experimental group. Nevertheless, you realize that there is always the potential for error no matter how careful a researcher tries to be. Would you state this circumstance as an assumption, as a limitation, or simply not refer to it in your paper? Why?

9. Consider a research project that you might wish to undertake. If you know of an assumption that you would probably need to make, write a statement describing it.

10. Consider a research project that you might wish to undertake. If you know of a limitation that you would probably have if you conducted the study, write a statement describing it. For the same study, describe a boundary to which the study would probably be delimited.

Chapter 8

Writing Method Sections

The section on methods contains a description of the physical steps taken to gather data. Typically, it begins with a description of the subjects and instrumentation (i.e., measuring tools).[1] Any procedures such as administration of experimental treatments should also be described here. Usually, it is better to overdescribe than underdescribe the methods employed, especially in the first draft of a report.

Clear, precise descriptions of methods accomplish two purposes: (1) they allow readers to visualize the procedures used, which is necessary if they are to understand your results fully and (2) they permit other researchers to replicate your study. Studies that cannot be replicated carry little or no weight in the scientific community.

In reports of completed research, use the past tense to describe methods; in proposals, use the future tense.

---

[1]See Guidelines 6.6 and 6.7 in Chapter 6 for additional information on describing instrumentation.

✓ *Guideline 8.1*

The subjects should be described in enough detail so that the reader can visualize the subjects.

In Example 8.1.A, the reader can visualize the subjects' gender, age, length of service, highest level of education, and managerial status. Notice that the subjects are referred to as *participants*; this is acceptable in journal articles. Writers of theses and dissertations should usually use the more commonly used term, *subjects*.

Example 8.1.A [2]

> Participants in this study were 150 full-time employees of a financial services organization that had undergone layoffs five to seven months prior to this study. All participants had been working for the company for at least nine months prior to the study. Forty-six percent of the participants were male and 54 percent were female. Their average age was 37.43 years, and their average length of service was 10.26 years. Nearly three-quarters of them had completed at least one year of college, and 56 percent reported that they held managerial positions.

In Example 8.1.B, the authors report the frequencies (i.e., numbers of cases) associated with each percentage; this is usually desirable.

---

[2] Brockner, Tyler, & Cooper-Schneider (1992, pp. 246-247)

Example 8.1.B [3]

Of the 531 employees in the sample, 292 (55 percent) were women and 239 (45 percent were men). The mean age of employees was 39.33 years (SD = 7.64), and 287 (54 percent) of the employees were white. Tenure in the organization averaged 16.96 years (SD = 7.28), and the average tenure in the current job was 3.77 years (SD = 2.52). Approximately 70 percent of the sample had attended college; 27 percent of the participants were college graduates. . . .

Tables such as that shown in Example 8.1.C make it easy for readers to compare two or more groups of subjects. [4]

Example 8.1.C [5]

Table 1
Demographic Characteristics of the Sample, Broken Down by Sex

Characteristic	Male managers (*n* = 795)	Female managers (*n* = 223)
Married	86%	45%
Children at home	62%	20%
Education		
Bachelor's degree	62%	59%
Graduate degree	22%	20%
Function		
Sales/marketing	37%	39%

[3] Igbaria & Greenhaus (1992, p. 482)
[4] Only a portion of the table is shown in the example.
[5] Stroh, Brett, & Reilly (1992, p. 253)

✓ *Guideline 8.2*

A population should be named and the method used to select the sample should be described.

Example 8.2.A illustrates this guideline.

Example 8.2.A [6]

> The sample for this study was 1,029 male and female managers who were transferred in 1987 or 1988 by 20 Fortune 500 corporations. These 20 companies represented eight industries: pharmaceutical and hospital supplies, communications, consumer products (food), professional and financial services, retailing, hotel management, chemicals, and manufacturing. Each company provided the names and addresses of all managers who had been transferred in 1987 and 1988. . . . Surveys were sent to 50 randomly selected managers from each firm.

The population in Example 8.2.A consists of all managers in certain corporations transferred during certain years. The sample was selected at *random*. When samples are selected at random, it is important to state this fact because (1) random selection is highly desirable and (2) unless a specific method of sampling is mentioned sophisticated readers will assume that a convenience sample was used, which is undesirable.

---

[6] Stroh, Brett, & Reilly (1992, p. 253)

✓ *Guideline 8.3*

If there was attrition, state the number of subjects who dropped out, the reasons for the attrition, if known, and information about the dropouts, if available.

Example 8.3.A illustrates this guideline.

Example 8.3.A

> The data for five of the subjects (two men and three women) were eliminated from the analysis because they failed to attend the final session, at which time the posttest was administered. These five subjects did not differ significantly from the remaining subjects in terms of age and socioeconomic status.

A common reason why subjects who were originally selected were not included in a study is the failure of some subjects to return questionnaires that were mailed to them. When this occurs, it is highly desirable to report the return rate in terms of the number of subjects and the corresponding percentage; it is desirable because a low return rate could result in a seriously biased sample while a high rate of return is a strength of a study. Readers should be given enough information so that they can identify important strengths *and* weaknesses of a study. In Example 8.3.B, the authors describe and evaluate the response rate to a mailed survey.

Example 8.3.B [7]

Of the 333 questionnaires mailed, seven were returned unopened because the firms were no longer in business. A total of 150 usable questionnaires were received for a response rate of 46% (150 out of 326). This compares favorably to other distribution channel surveys, which commonly have response rates between 16 and 47%. . . .

One measure was available to examine whether or not respondents were representative of chemical distributors. It was "major product lines carried" by the sample frame. A chi-square test found no significant difference between respondents and non-respondents in terms of 18 major product lines carried. . . . Based on this one measure, the sample is representative of the chemical distributors surveyed.

✓ *Guideline 8.4*

If an unpublished instrument was used, describe it in detail.

The authors of Example 8.4.A followed this guideline by providing the general description shown in the example and then providing a table in the article in which the actual items for each of the five appraisal guidelines are shown.

---

[7] Narus & Guimaraes (1987, p. 46)

Example 8.4.A[8]

> The performance appraisal principles for this study were measured by means of a questionnaire designed to measure the predominant perception of management style within a given country. The questionnaire (using a seven-point bi-polar rating scale) was. . . . [The] items were related to the generally accepted performance appraisal principles of (a) formality of structures and controls; (b) individual vs. team development; (c) employee involvement in the appraisal process; (d) intrinsic vs. extrinsic rewards; and (e) frequency of performance feedback.

Because the questionnaire in Example 8.4.A contains only eight items, the authors included all of the items in the body of the report. Longer instruments should be described in general in the method section and included in appendices in theses and dissertations. If the instrument is included in an appendix, be sure to mention this fact in the method section.

✓ *Guideline 8.5*

If a published instrument was used, briefly describe the traits that it was designed to measure, its format, scoring procedures, and the possible range of score values.

---

[8]Vance, McClaine, Boje, & Stage (1992, p. 317)

The authors of Example 8.5.A followed this guideline.

Example 8.5.A[9]

> Direction of information processing was measured with procedures used in prior research (Petty, Harkins, & Williams, 1980). . . . Specifically, subjects were given 3 min to write the thoughts (cognitive responses) that occurred to them as they read the advertisement for the target product (Chaing VCR). Then, after writing their thoughts, subjects were asked to label their cognitive responses as negative (–), positive (+), or neutral (0). This procedure has been used in previous research (Harkins & Petty, 1987). Upon completion of the experiment, research assistants, unaware of the research hypotheses, counted the total number of positive and negative cognitive responses from each subject. The direction of information processing was calculated by subtracting the number of negative cognitive responses from the number of positive cognitive responses for each subject. . . .

Note that the authors provide references that contain additional information on the measurement procedure. This is highly desirable. In a thesis or dissertation, students should also summarize the information contained in such references.

---

[9] Gotlieb & Dubinsky (1991, pp. 544-545)

✓ Guideline 8.6

In theses and dissertations, information on reliability and validity should be described in detail; in journal articles, a brief summary of information on reliability and validity is usually sufficient, and it may be sufficient only to refer to a published source of information on these topics if the instrument is well known and in widespread use.

It is suggested that writers of theses and dissertations provide detailed information on these matters in order to demonstrate that they are fully familiar with the instruments that they have used. A thesis is, in part, a test of the ability to be thorough in describing the methods employed in a study.

✓ Guideline 8.7

Physical procedures, equipment, and other mechanical matters should be described in sufficient detail so that the study can be replicated.

Example 8.7.A describes the stimulus materials that were shown to a group of subjects. The four interiors could have been described in more detail; however, journal space is limited and, thus, it is problematic as to how detailed a description should be.

The descriptions in Example 8.7.A are probably sufficient for a journal article, especially since the address of the first author is given in the article, permitting correspondence concerning the slides. In a thesis or dissertation, prints made from the color slides probably should be appended.

Example 8.7.A[10]

> Slides of pictures of four restaurant interiors were used for the study. Pictures were obtained from interior design and hospitality trade magazines. Each picture included the ceiling, floor, and at least two walls of the interior of the restaurant. Each restaurant picture also included tables, chairs, tablecloths, and table settings but did not include food or any people (whether employees or customers). . . . Restaurant 1 had exposed brick walls, pastel colors and a clouds and sky motif on the ceiling. Restaurant 2 was of a strikingly contemporary architectural style, with unusual lighting and black accents. Restaurant 3 was a restaurant/bar which used glass, mirror, and brass extensively. Restaurant 4 was a traditional room with high ceilings, patterned carpet, and many potted palms.

Concluding Comments

Considerable subjectivity enters into the decision as to how much detail to provide; in most cases, authors of published

---

[10] Burns & Caughey (1992, pp. 108–109)

research do not provide every detail of their procedures. Instead, they try to provide enough to permit a reasonably close replication.

Exercise for Chapter 8

1. Locate a description of subjects that is highly detailed in a journal article, thesis, or dissertation. Bring it to class for discussion.

2. Locate a description of subjects that lacks sufficient detail. Copy it and briefly describe other types of information that might have been included to give a better picture of the subjects.

3. Examine the description of subjects in five sources. In how many did the authors explicitly name a population? In how many did the authors state that random selection from a population was used? In how many did the authors state that there was attrition and, if any, in how many were the reasons for the attrition given?

4. Examine the description of the instrumentation in the five sources that you used for question 3. In how many was an unpublished instrument used? If any, copy the description and indicate whether you believe that the description is sufficiently detailed.

5. Examine the description of procedures in the five sources that you used for question 3. Copy the one that is most detailed. Briefly describe whether you think it is sufficiently detailed and why.

Chapter 9

Writing Analysis and Results Sections

The analysis and results section usually follows the section on methods. In a proposal, the proposed method of analysis should be described; the anticipated results may also be discussed.

✔ Guideline 9.1

Organize the analysis and results section around the research hypotheses (or purposes or questions) stated in the introduction; describe the analysis and results for the first hypothesis first, then describe them for the second hypothesis, and so on.

If you presented a numbered list of hypotheses earlier in the report, refer to the content of each hypothesis and its number in order to identify it. Example 9.1.A illustrates this guideline; it shows the beginnings of the first two paragraphs in the results section.

Example 9.1.A [1]

> The first hypothesis predicted that informal protégés would report receiving more career-related and psychosocial functions than formal protégés. The mean scores for protégés reports of functions provided by their mentors are provided in. . .
>
> The second hypothesis predicted differences among informal protégés, formal protégés, and nonmentored individuals on organizational socialization (Hypothesis 2a), intrinsic job satisfaction (Hypothesis 2b), and salary (Hypothesis 2c). The group means and standard deviations for these outcome measures are shown in Table 2. The pattern of means is. . .

✓ *Guideline 9.2*

Standard statistical procedures need only be named; you do not need to show the formulas.

Likewise, it is usually unnecessary to name the particular computer program used in the analysis.

---

[1] Chao, Walz, & Gardner (1992, p. 627)

✔ *Guideline 9.3*

Raw scores are usually not reported; only the statistics based on them are reported.

The major exception to this guideline is when only a very small number of subjects was studied. Also, in a thesis or dissertation, where space is not at a premium, raw scores may be given in an appendix, although this is not always required.

✔ *Guideline 9.4*

Present descriptive statistics first, usually starting with measures of central tendency and variability (or, for categorical data, starting with frequencies and percentages).

For each set of scores, provide information on central tendency and variability (usually the means and standard deviations) before presenting correlation coefficients, if any, and the results of inferential tests. For example, correlation coefficients may provide direct information on a given research hypothesis; even when this is the case, report measures of central tendency and variability first. These measures will show your reader what the average subject was like and how variable the group was.

For categorical data, present frequencies and percentages before presenting the results of inferential tests such as the chi square test.

✓ *Guideline 9.5*

Organize large amounts of data in tables and give each table a number and a descriptive title (i.e., caption).

Each title usually should name the statistics presented in the table and refer to the variables that were measured. The title in Example 9.5.A names the statistic (i.e., the mean) and the variables (i.e., advertising response, comprehension, and positioning). Notice that the title does *not* end with a period mark.

Example 9.5.A [2]

Mean Advertising Response by Comprehension and Positioning

In Example 9.5.B, the term *intercorrelations* refers to the statistics. Because there were 15 variables in the title, they are not named but referred to as *variables* in the title, which is appropriate when there are many variables; of course, the names of the variables are listed in the body of the table. In this example, the phrase *from Rural Backgrounds* is important because the next table in the article shows the statistics for the same variables for a sample of females from urban backgrounds.

Example 9.5.B [3]

Intercorrelations Between Variables for the Career Orientation Model for Females from Urban Backgrounds

---

[2] Jaffe, Jamieson, & Berger (1992, p. 30)
[3] Poole, Langan-Fox, & Omodei (1991, p. 999)

Table numbers and titles usually are placed immediately above the tables. Titles do not need to be long to be effective, as illustrated in Example 9.5.C. Notice the use of a footnote to explain the source of the data and the use of zero as a place holder for the two entries that are less than one (i.e., the statistics for disciplinary grievances with positive outcomes).

Example 9.5.C[4]

Table 1

Means and Standard Deviations for Absenteeism and Grievance Activity

Variable	*M*	*SD*
Disciplinary grievances		
No. filed	1.63	1.38
Negative outcomes	1.13	1.14
Positive outcomes	0.50	0.75
Policy Grievances		
No. filed	5.19	4.43
Negative outcomes	2.90	3.36
Positive outcomes	2.39	2.00
Absenteeism	236.53	42.33

Note: N = 96. Data are based on monthly tallies

---

[4]Klass, Heneman, & Olson (1991, p. 821)

✔ *Guideline 9.6*

In the text, describe the main conclusions to be reached based on each table and point out highlights that the reader may otherwise overlook. You do not need to discuss each entry in a table.

To describe all of the entries would be redundant. Example 9.6.A shows the description of the table shown in Example 9.5.C. Comparison of the description with the table reveals that the description points out trends using approximations while the table provides the precise statistics that identified the trends.

Example 9.6.A [5]

Monthly means and standard deviations of the variables are shown in Table 1. On average, there were approximately 236 absences per month, though there was considerable variability around this number. Three times as many policy grievances as disciplinary grievances were filed. . . . On average, policy grievances resulted in approximately equal numbers of positive and negative outcomes. Disciplinary grievances, alternatively, yielded more than twice as many negative outcomes as positive ones.

For a table containing 16 statistics, the authors provide a brief but effective description shown in Example 9.6.B.

---

[5] Klass, Heneman, & Olson (1991, p. 821)

Example 9.6.B [6]

> Results of the analysis showed that layout style can positively affect reader response to business-to-business advertisements. Rebus ads were found to produce the best results, followed by Ayer #1, Parallel Panels, then Miscellaneous. Table 1 shows the actual dependent measures for the various layout styles.

For a table containing 32 numerical values, the authors provided the brief description in Example 9.6.C. In this example, the authors use shorthand terms indicated in all capital letters, which were, of course, defined earlier in the report.

Example 9.6.C [7]

> Table 2 presents the empirical results. The first estimation was for sample 1, the seventy-six students who completed the microeconomics course sequence. With the exception of LECTURE, all the variables had the anticipated signs and were statistically significant at either the 1 percent level (GPA and BREAK) or the 5 percent level (STATUS, MATH, and MGRADE) using a one-tailed t test. LECTURE had the expected sign but was statistically insignificant. The coefficient of determination was .307, and the F statistic was 6.532.

Notice that the authors refer to the tables by number. Do not use phrases such as "The table below indicates" because you cannot be certain of the placement of a table when your report is typed or typeset.

---

[6] Chamblee & Sandler (1992, pp. 42–43)
[7] Raimondo, Esposito, & Gershenberg (1990, 376–377)

✓ *Guideline 9.7*

Statistical figures (i.e., drawings such as pie charts and bar graphs) should be professionally drawn and used sparingly in journal articles.

Figures may be used to organize and describe data; however, they usually take up more space than a corresponding statistical table would. Because space in journals is expensive and because the primary audience for journal articles is sophisticated in interpreting statistics, figures should be used sparingly. In theses and dissertations, where space is not limited, they may be used more frequently.

In nonscientific business writing, figures are frequently used to capture the audience's attention and to make statistics less threatening and more comprehensible for readers with little training in statistics.

✓ *Guideline 9.8*

All tables and figures in a report should be referred to in the body of the text.

It is the writer's obligation to point out how the tables and figures relate to the material presented in the body of the text. Tables and figures that do not deserve mention in the text should be deleted from a report.

✓ Guideline 9.9

Statistical symbols should be underlined or italicized.

Example 9.9.A

> The mean of the experimental group was significantly higher than the mean of the control group ($t = 2.310$, $df = 10$, $p < .05$, two tailed).

In Example 9.9.A, the three statistical symbols are italicized. If you do not have the ability to italicize, underline the symbols; typesetters recognize underlining as a direction to italicize.

✓ Guideline 9.10

Use the proper case for each statistical symbol.

Many letters in statistics have two meanings, which are differentiated by their case. For example, a lower-case f stands for "frequency," but an upper-case F is an inferential statistic used in significance testing.

✓ *Guideline 9.11*

Numerals that start sentences and that are less than 12 usually should be spelled out.[8]

The primary exceptions to this rule are when authors refer to elements in a numbered set such as "Chapter 1" or "Guideline 2" or when presenting precise numerical results such as $M = 2.11$.

✓ *Guideline 9.12*

The term *significance* often should be modified with an adjective—either *statistical* or *practical*.

The term *statistical significance* refers to the reliability of the results (i.e., it refers to the question, "are the results reliable in light of sampling errors, which occur as a result of random sampling?") Often, a small difference that is of *statistical* significance (i.e., is reliable) has no *practical* significance (i.e., is too small to be of concern in everyday affairs).

The guideline does not need to be followed when the context makes it clear which type of significance is being discussed. For example, in a paragraph in which the results of significance tests are being reported, it is often clear from the context that practical matters are not being discussed. When both are discussed in the same section or paragraph, the adjectives should be used. The authors of Example 9.12.A have in their article a paragraph in which

---

[8] There is some variation among style manuals on this guideline.

they discuss both the practical and statistical significance of their results. They conclude that paragraph with the sentence shown in the example.

Example 9.12.A[9]

Thus, this relationship is statistically and practically significant.

✓ *Guideline 9.13*

Qualitative results need to be organized and the organization made clear to the reader.

In qualitative studies, quantitative data often are deemphasized. Instead, the authors usually emphasize major trends and themes that emerged from subjective analyses[10] of data such as transcribed interviews. The discussion of such results should be organized; consider using subheadings to guide the reader in the discussion.

In discussing the qualitative results of 27 semistructured interviews (i.e., interviews in which there is some standardization from subject to subject but in which the interviewer is free to explore issues that emerge during the interviews), the authors of Example 9.12.A organized their results under specific headings, some of which are shown in the example in italics along with some of the results. Notice that the author is blending some simple statistics

---

[9]Klaas, Heneman, & Olson (1991, p. 821)

[10]The term *subjective analysis* is used here to distinguish this type of analysis from a highly objective type such as scoring multiple-choice items and computing an average.

such as percentages with interviewees' comments, which were selected by the author to illustrate the main findings.

Example 9.13.A [11]

> *What is stress? Managers' Responses*
>
> One of the interviewees commented, "[It's] like a grey elephant. You know one when you see one but it's difficult to define!" Fifty percent of the interviewees identified the individual as the source of stress. . . .
>
> *What is Counselling? Managers' Responses*
>
> Nearly half the interviewees mentioned "listening", and just over one-third named "talking". . . . It was often considered to be about communication, in which managers, as well as employees, would make a substantial contribution to the discussion. This is reflected in the prominence of "guiding", "advising" or "helping" in the responses.

An investigator who employed open-ended interviews reported results using headings such as: "Two types of part-time jobs," "Job demands," "Pay and benefits," and "Turnover."[12] Such headings help readers understand the results.

Exercise for Chapter 9

1. Examine the results sections of two published articles. Determine whether the authors followed Guideline 9.4. Be prepared to discuss your findings in class.

---

[11] Wheeler & Lyon (1992, pp. 51–53)
[12] Tilly (1992, pp. 333–336)

2. Locate a statistical table in a published article that you think has a good title (i.e., caption). Make a photocopy of it and bring it to class for discussion. Be prepared to discuss whether the author named both the statistics and the variables in the title.

3. Locate a statistical table in a published article and discuss whether it communicates the statistics more effectively than would be possible if the statistics were integrated with the text.

4. For the table you located for Question 2, copy the discussion of it. Be prepared to discuss whether the author followed Guideline 9.6.

5. Locate a statistical figure in a published article and discuss whether presentation in the form of a table would have been as effective.

Notes:

Chapter 10

Writing Discussion Sections

The following are guidelines for writing the last section of the body of a journal article or the last chapter of a thesis or dissertation. The most common heading for this section is *discussion*; occasionally authors use the heading *conclusion*.

In very brief journal articles, the results and discussion sections are sometimes integrated into a single section.

✓ Guideline 10.1

A brief summary of the study may be included in the discussion section of a journal article; a long, detailed summary may be required in a thesis or dissertation.

At the end of a long journal article, a summary is desirable but may be omitted in a brief one. When a summary is included, some authors use the heading *summary and discussion* to identify the discussion section of a journal article or chapter of a thesis or dissertation.

✓ *Guideline 10.2*

Consider beginning the discussion section with a restatement of the research purposes, questions, or hypotheses.

The restatement usually should be *verbatim* in theses, dissertations, and long journal articles. In short journal articles, it may be sufficient to remind readers of the general purpose; the authors of Example 10.2.A illustrate this. They tested seven specific hypotheses but began their discussion section with a statement of their general purpose. Notice that this naturally leads to a summary of the findings (i.e., results) relating to this purpose.

Example 10.2.A[1]

> The purpose of this article was to test the common notion that Japanese operating managers adhere to 'quality is free' philosophies, while the operating philosophies of US managers are grounded in economic conformance ideas. First, our findings indicate that. . .

The authors of Example 10.2.B also began their discussion section by reminding readers of their general purpose.

---

[1] Reitsperger & Daniel (1991, p. 595)

Example 10.2.B [2]

> In this article, we developed three empirical models to study different aspects of sales-force compensation structures. Guided by theories from several disciplines, we specified relationships that we estimated using sales-force data from. . .

✓ *Guideline 10.3*

Explicitly state whether the research hypotheses were supported. If research questions were stated instead of hypotheses, explicitly answer the questions.

Guideline 10.3 is illustrated in Examples 10.3.A and 10.3.B.

Example 10.3.A [3]

> The results of discriminant analysis supported all but one of the hypotheses. For all four CVS dimensions, the scores of the Hong Kong managers fell between or were no more than equivalent to the scores of the U.S. or PRC managers. This finding is consistent with our initial hypothesis and suggests that the thinking of Hong Kong managers is influenced by the Eastern cultural heritage and their exposure to Western ways of business.

In Example 10.3.B, the authors refer to social learning theory, which they used in their introduction to provide a rationale for their hypothesis. In the discussion section it is appropriate to

---

[2] Coughlan & Narasimhan (1992, p. 117)
[3] Ralston, Gustafson, Elsass, Cheung, & Terpstra (1992, p. 669)

remind readers of the origin of or basis for the hypothesis in the discussion section.

Example 10.3.B [4]

> Consistent with the research hypothesis, it is shown that, after controlling for regional effects, peer group characteristics predict individual job performance beyond individual characteristics. These results are consistent with a social learning theory conceptualization of individual behavior as the result of an interaction between the person and the situation.

✓ *Guideline 10.4*

Highlights of the results should be described in the discussion section.

This guideline is illustrated in Example 10.4.A., in which the authors examined women's participation in union leadership. Notice that the authors do not state precise statistics but, rather, use phrases such as "less well represented" and "nearly proportional," which are based on precise statistics in their results section. Although it is acceptable to restate some key statistics, it would be redundant to restate them all in the discussion section.

---

[4]Baratta & McManus (1992, p. 1707)

Example 10.4.A[5]

First, our findings, in conjunction with those of previous studies, suggest that women are less well represented in leadership at the national level than at the local level. Second, although our survey of officials at AFL-CIO-affiliated locals in Massachusetts shows that women fill leadership positions in those locals in numbers nearly proportional to their membership, our results also show that women are more commonly found in relatively marginal positions than in influential positions. . .

The authors of Example 10.4.B also summarized their results in several paragraphs of their discussion section. A portion is shown here to illustrate how results are highlighted and not restated in detail.

Example 10.4.B[6]

Specifically, although females tended to perceive the behaviors as being more sexually harassing than did males, this difference was large only when there was a relatively large status difference between the instigator of the behavior and the recipient. Gender differences tended to be small when the difference in status was small. The largest gender differences were found. . .

---

[5] Melcher, Eichstedt, Eriksen, & Clawson (1992, p. 277)
[6] Sheffey & Tindale (1992, p. 1514)

✓ *Guideline 10.5*

Explicitly state the implications of the results in the discussion section.

Implications are usually cast in terms of actions that individuals should take based on the results of a study. There may also be implications for theory development.

The authors of Example 10.5.A provide a statement of the implications of their results for public policy makers.

Example 10.5.A [7]

> In general it appears that buyers (even when uninformed) can be wise and adopt strategies that minimize the possibility of their being cheated. This argument is one that may be of interest to makers of public policy. Clearly, low prices are desirable from a consumer welfare standpoint only if such low prices do not result in the complete disappearance of high-quality sellers . . . Therefore, an attempt to depress market prices as a means of ensuring consumer welfare may actually result in a loss of welfare because of the more than commensurate reduction in the quality of delivered products.

Stating the implications of a study at the end of the discussion section often provides a strong ending to an article. Example 10.5.B shows part of the last two paragraphs of an article; these paragraphs were set off with their own subheading of *practical implications*.

---

[7] Rao & Bergen (1992, p. 421)

Example 10.5.B [8]

    The results suggest that fairness is an important component of job satisfaction among the personnel sampled in the present study. In other words, employees perceiving fairness in pay and promotions were more likely to feel satisfied with their jobs than employees perceiving less fairness or unfairness. This suggests the utility of supervisors' and managers' explaining and discussing personnel outcomes and, when appropriate, emphasizing the fairness of those outcomes and the procedures leading to those outcomes. Supervisor articulation of. . .

    Notice that in Example 10.5.B the authors use the phrase "among the personnel sampled in the present study." Even though they used a sample consisting of several thousand subjects in a variety of occupations such as nonmedical hospital employees, printers, and FAA accounting staff, the authors are reminding readers that the implications may not hold for all types of employees.

    If you have conducted a pilot study as a project for a research class, you may wish to hedge in your statement of implications by beginning the statement with a cautionary note such as that shown in Example 10.5.C.

Example 10.5.C

    If the results obtained in this pilot study are confirmed in more definitive studies, the following implications should be considered by. . .

---

[8] Witt, & Nye (1992, p. 916)

✔ *Guideline 10.6*

Important strengths and limitations should be mentioned in the discussion section.

Strengths and limitations of the research methodology should first be discussed in the section on methods. Important strengths and limitations that affect the interpretation of data should be mentioned again in the discussion section in order to help readers determine how much caution to use in applying the results.

The authors of Example 10.6.A included a subsection entitled *limitations and future research* within their discussion section; in their article they report on two studies that they conducted.

Example 10.6.A[9]

> . . . the generalizability of our results is subject to question. For instance, the observed effects are likely to vary across product classes, particularly if different product classes reveal their quality-related properties to differing degrees. . . .
>
> Clearly, our inability to completely replicate the findings from study 1 in study 2 is a source of concern. It would have been gratifying. . .

[9] Rao & Sieben (1992, p. 268)

✓ *Guideline 10.7*

If you issue a call for further research on a problem, provide the reader with specific guidance.

Few studies are conclusive; additional research on important problems is usually needed. Therefore, it is of little value merely to tell a reader that more research is recommended. The reasons why more research is needed and the form that it might take should be stated.

The authors of Example 10.7.A stated four specific avenues for future research, portions of which are shown in the example.

Example 10.7.A[10]

. . . we examined the influence of prices on three aspects of consumers' cognitive process. In future research, the impact of other variables on aspects of consumers' cognitive process should be investigated. For example, this research did not explore the effect of cognitive responses on behavioral intentions. . . . Second, the present experiment employed college students; future work might use samples from diverse populations to test the generalizability of the results. . . . Fourth, participants in the experiment had experience with the product of interest (a VCR). Subsequent empirical work might include subjects who have varying degrees of experience. . . .

Example 10.7.B shows two of the five research questions that were suggested for future research by the authors of a study of examinations in a management course.

---

[10]Gotlieb & Dubinsky (1991, p. 548)

Example 10.7.B [11]

Can the multiple-choice test results of low-performing management students be improved when they are encouraged and even "taught" to follow the suggested study model?

How do students who fit the success profile identified here perform in other upper-level management courses that are not taught in large-lecture formats?

Students who are looking for suitable research hypotheses or questions to explore in a class project, thesis, or dissertation are encouraged to examine discussion sections, where experts often provide specific suggestions for future research.

✓ *Guideline 10.8*

Point out consistencies and inconsistencies of the current results with those in the literature cited earlier in the report.

Application of this guideline reminds readers of the scientific context within which the study was conducted and helps them see how the current results contribute to the literature. This is illustrated in Example 10.8.A.

Example 10.8.A [12]

. . . recruiting practices had a significant effect on all five measures of applicant reactions to the initial employment interview. Their effect on

---

[11] Schermerhorn, Gardner, & Dresdow (1992, p.442)
[12] Powell (1991, p. 68)

the likelihood of job offer and job acceptance was significant even when perceptions of job attributes were controlled. Thus, the results added to the sole support previously offered by Harris and Fink (1987) for an effect of recruiting practices on applicant reactions when job attributes are simultaneously examined. However, the size of this effect for likelihood of job acceptance, although statistically significant, could still be regarded as small.

Example 10.8.B also illustrates how results may be related to previous literature in the discussion section.

Example 10.8.B [13]

The results concur with Adams's (1965) claim that job status or status symbols are important considerations in determining feelings of inequity and that discomfort is aroused when a person's outcome/input ratio is disturbed. When workers perceive inequity to be to their own disadvantage, they express more negative attitudes and behave in a fashion opposed to organizational goals. Hence, the present study expands the already well-known influence of monetary rewards on inequity to the area of promotion decisions (e.g., Greenberg, 1988; Greenberg & Ornstein, 1983; Mowday, 1987).

✔ *Guideline 10.9*

It is acceptable to speculate on the meaning of the results.

---

[13] Schwarzwald, Koslowsky, & Shalit (1992, p. 513)

When authors speculate, they are going beyond the data in their interpretation of their results. In the discussion section, authors should clearly identify statements that are speculative in nature. The safest way to do this is to introduce speculative statements with a phrase such as "It is interesting to speculate on. . ." This is especially recommended for students whose instructors will want to know if they know the difference between data-based conclusions and speculation.

In Example 10.9.A, the authors indicate the speculative nature of their statement by using the term *possible reasons*, which is perfectly acceptable.

Example 10.9.A[14]

> Finally, we will address possible reasons for the fact that the four original career path dimensions addressed in our hypotheses explained a comparatively small amount of variance in the career success measures and had little effect on the gender-success relations. One possibility is that differences in career success may be less attributable to career path differences among MBSs than among less well-educated work populations. For example, much of the prior discussion of career ladder differences. . .

✓ *Guideline 10.10*

It is usually inappropriate to introduce new data or new references to literature in the discussion and conclusion section.

---

[14] Cox & Harquail (1991, p. 72)

The final section of the body of the report should be used to summarize and interpret what was presented earlier. The introduction of new data or references distracts from this purpose.

✓ *Guideline 10.11*

Provide subheadings within long discussion sections.

Subheadings help readers understand the structure of discussion sections and are especially appropriate in long, complicated discussions. Example 10.11.A shows both the major and minor subheadings in a long discussion section in a journal article. Notice that the authors centered the heading *Discussion and Conclusions* and left-justified the major subheadings; the minor subheadings were italicized and included in the body of the paragraphs.[15] Also notice how spacing is used to set off the various sections. The headings in the example are underlined to help you identify them; they were *not* underlined in the article.

Example 10.11.A[16]

DISCUSSION AND CONCLUSIONS

Summary

The research reported here is an initial attempt at understanding whether and when buyers knowingly pay prices that are higher than justified by the. . .

---

[15] This form for heading and subheadings is recommended for students who do not have a style manual that treats this issue.
[16] Rao & Bergen (1992, pp. 418–421)

<u>Speculation Regarding Reputation Effect</u>

Our results suggest that, for experience products, buyers grant price premiums to reputationless sellers to a greater degree. . .

<u>Buyer Behavior Implications</u>

While our data consist of organizational buyers responses, the consumer behavior analogy is apparent when we consider. . .

<u>Limitations and Future Research</u>

Alternative Approaches. As we mentioned earlier, we have adopted one of a variety of approaches that can be used to motivate the existence of price. . . .

Measurement Issues. Achieving high reliability values in survey research of practicing managers using constructs that do not have a long measurement tradition is difficult, yet. . .

In Example 10.11.B the first two subheadings refer to key variables in the authors' study. Again, the headings are underlined in the example to help you identify them, but they were *not* underlined in the original.

Example 10.11.B [17]

DISCUSSION

This article addressed two principal issues. First, the study examined the limits of acceptable price ranges of subjects who differed in. . .

---

[17] Rao & Sieben (1992, pp. 267–269)

Price Limits

The finding that low-knowledge subjects systematically displayed lower price limits than moderately or highly knowledgeable subjects is a finding that is consistent. . .

Information-Examination Patterns

With regard to the relative examination of extrinsic versus intrinsic information, the results of the study are consistent with the . . .

Limitations and Future Research

In the tradition of previous research. . . , prior knowledge was premeasured and not manipulated. While this does not rule out rival hypotheses. . .

Concluding Comment

A discussion section that reviews the results of the study, gives suggestions for future research, and suggests implications for specific users provides a strong ending to a research report.

Exercise for Chapter 10

1. Locate a journal article with a discussion section that contains a summary. (Note: It is common to put the summary, if any, at the very beginning of the discussion section or at the very end.) Be prepared to discuss the adequacy of the summary, keeping in mind that most summaries should be relatively short.

2. Locate a journal article in which the implications of the results are explicitly stated in the discussion and conclusions section. Be prepared to discuss whether the implications are clearly derived from the data presented.

3. Locate a journal article in which the author points out consistencies and inconsistencies of his or her results with research he/she cited earlier in the article. Be prepared to discuss whether they are clearly stated.

4. Locate a journal article in which the discussion section has subheadings. Copy it and be prepared to discuss whether the subheadings help readers follow the discussion.

5. Read a journal article but do not read the discussion and conclusion section. Write a discussion and conclusion section for it and then compare your material with that provided by the author(s) of the article.

Chapter 11

Writing Abstracts

An abstract is a summary that is placed before the introduction in a journal article, thesis, or dissertation. Its major purpose is to give readers an overview that helps them determine whether they wish to read the entire document. Usually journals and universities put word limits on abstracts, often about 75 to 150 words for journal articles; limits for abstracts of theses and dissertations often are more generous.

✔ Guideline 11.1

Highlights of the results usually should be included in an abstract.

In Example 11.1.A, two of the three sentences describe results. Notice that the results are described in general terms (i.e., "superior to" and "small and statistically insignificant difference") rather than with specific statistics.

Example 11.1.A[1]

> In two experiments, the authors manipulated the audience's level of involvement in processing an advertisement and whether the advertisement was open-ended (i.e., did not include an explicit conclusion) or closed-ended. Results of both experiments show the open-ended advertisement to be superior to the closed-ended one for an involved audience in terms of brand attitude, purchase intention, and choice, whereas only a small and statistically insignificant difference between the two types of advertisements is found for the uninvolved audience. Moreover, the second experiment shows that the choice advantage of the open-ended ad for the involved audience persisted when measured one week later.

The author of example 11.1.B also stresses his results, providing a lettered list of them. Notice that he introduces the list with the phrase "The results *suggest* that" [italics added]. Terms such as *suggest, indicate,* or *point to* almost always are more appropriate than *prove,* which suggests that the results are conclusive—a type of result that, strictly speaking, never is obtained through empirical research. In an abstract for a highly definitive study (i.e., a study with an excellent sample, tight controls over potential extraneous variables, and highly reliable and valid instruments), an author might be justified in using terms such as *very strongly suggest* or *almost certainly.*

---

[1] Sawyer & Howard (1991, p. 467)

Example 11.1.B [2]

This study examines the process of upward influence in a variety of strategic decisions. The study provides a list of categories and supporting data for the agents, methods, perceived outcomes, and perceived causes of success and failure of upward influence interactions that impact upon the strategic decision-making process in organizations. The results suggest that: (a) middle-level managers (MLMs) deal directly with their superiors and use rational or persuasive arguments in their upward influence interactions in strategic decisions; (2) MLMs are very successful in their influence interactions and attribute their successes to internal causes; (3) MLMs and their superiors view the influence episode similarly; and (4) upward influence activity in strategic decisions is quite similar to upward influence activity in non-strategic decisions. The study also examines individual and organizational factors that are associated with success and failure in influence activity in strategic decision-making.

✓ *Guideline 11.2*

Highlights of the methodology usually should be mentioned, especially if the methodology is superior to that used in previous studies.

In the second sentence of Example 11.2.A, the authors point out methodological weaknesses in previous studies; in the third

---

[2] Schilit (1990, p. 435)

sentence, they indicate that the weaknesses were avoided in their study.

Example 11.2.A [3]

Many advertisers have argued that 15-second television commercials (:15s) should be used only to reinforce effects created by longer commercials. However, this recommendation is based on studies that have several weaknesses, including use of single exposure levels, established commercials, and learning as the primary dependent variable. The authors report the findings of a laboratory experiment in which they compared the effectiveness of :15s and :30s by using novel commercials with different message appeals (informational vs. emotional), exposing subjects multiple times, and employing multiple dependent variables. They find that informational :15s are as effective as informational :30s in several situations and can be used as stand-alone units. They also show that emotional :30s are superior to emotional :15s in influencing a viewer's learning of brand name and attitude. The reasons for and the implications of these findings are considered.

In Example 11.2.B, the first four sentences deal with methodological issues (i.e., subjects and instrumentation). Notice that the authors name the precise number of subjects; this is acceptable but usually not necessary.

Example 11.2.B [4]

Nine male and ten female managers in a low stress group and ten male and ten female managers in a high stress group were studied.

---

[3] Singh & Cole (1993, p. 91)
[4] McDonald & Korabik (1991, p. 185)

They described stressful work-related situations they had experienced and how they coped with them. The revised Ways of Coping Checklist was completed for each situation described. A work stressors questionnaire was used to assess additional types of stressors experienced. Women were more likely than men to report that prejudice and discrimination and work/family interfaces were sources of stress. Male and female managers did not differ in the ways they coped with work-related problems. But, women were more likely to cope with their feelings about the problems by talking to others, whereas men were more likely to engage in a distracting nonwork activity. Those in high and low stress groups differed only in their use of "Wishful Thinking" as a way of coping.

✓ *Guideline 11.3*

Reference to the research hypotheses or purposes may be made.

The authors of Example 11.3.A begin their abstract with a description of their research purposes.

Example 11.3.A [5]

The purpose of this study was to explore the relationship between communication and productivity. Specifically, we had two aims: (a) to determine employee perceptions of the impact of eight dimensions of communication satisfaction on productivity, and (b) to understand how the type of organization may moderate the link

---

[5] Clampitt & Downs (1993, p. 5)

between communication and productivity. Two businesses, representative of service and manufacturing organizations, were investigated by administering the Communication Satisfaction Questionnaire and interviewing all employees. The results showed that communication was perceived to have an impact on productivity that varied in both kind and magnitude. Moreover, a number of intriguing differences emerged between these two companies. The findings suggest that the link between communication and productivity is more complex than previously assumed.

Notice that the authors of Example 11.3.A describe these elements, in order, in their abstract:

1. research purposes (or hypotheses)
2. methodology
3. results (or analysis and results)

This arrangement is recommended when space permits all of them to be covered. Of course, there will be exceptions; for example, if an innovative or greatly improved methodology has been used, this should be emphasized and an explicit statement of research hypotheses or purposes may be omitted in order to make room for the discussion of methodology. In almost all cases, some indication of the results should be included.

The author of Example 11.3.B used the same arrangement as the authors of Example 11.3.A.. Because Example 11.3.B is the abstract of a doctoral dissertation, it is longer than that permitted by journal editors, and it is divided into paragraphs; abstracts for journal articles are usually a single paragraph. In Example 11.3.B, only the beginning of each paragraph is shown and the numbers in brackets were added to help you identify the three basic elements in it: [1] hypothesis, [2] methodology, [3] method of analysis and results.

Example 11.3.B [6]

[1] The objective of this research was to test the hypothesis that a relationship exists between the Human Resource Management practices of small manufacturing companies and the performance of their organizations as measured by sales per employee. [2] To attain this objective, a questionnaire was distributed to owners and managers of small manufacturing companies in the state of Alabama. A total of 152 firms generated the data . . .

On the questionnaires, the owners and managers provided their perceptions of the value of the contribution made by. . . They rated each of thirteen. . .

[3] Owner responses were analyzed using discriminant analysis and analysis of variance tests. No statistically significant relationship was found between. . .

Some significant relationships were found. The size of the firm (using number of employees) was related to the perceived. . .

This research found no relationship between the perceived value of the Human Resource Management practices used by small manufacturing companies in Alabama and their success. It suggests other causal factors and questions. . . .

✔ *Guideline 11.4*

It is sometimes appropriate to point out the significance of the topic in an abstract.

---

[6]Gulbro (1992, pp. 216A–217A)

The significance of some topics is more readily apparent than others—and more readily apparent to some intended audiences than others. The decision as to how much emphasis to place on the significance of a topic, given the limited number of words allowed in abstracts, is a subjective matter. The authors of Example 11.4.A began their abstract by describing the significance of their topic and a gap in the literature. The rest of the abstract (not shown here) summarizes the methods used and results.

Example 11.4.A[7]

> The increasing need for integration and the rapid growth of online systems have made telecommunications a vital part of management information systems (MIS). In search of competitive advantage, organizations make significant investments in telecommunication. Telecommunications management is becoming a top priority of information systems executives. The MIS literature suggests that steering committees are effective means of managing information systems. However, there is no information on how steering committees impact the management of telecommunications . . . .

✓ *Guideline 11.5*

It is sometimes appropriate to summarize the implications of the results.

---

[7]Torkzadeh & Xia (1992, p. 187)

Including a summary of the implications is especially appropriate when the results of the study suggest implications that may lead to major changes in business practices.

In the second paragraph of Example 11.5.A, the authors summarize their *recommendations* (i.e., implications) based on the results of their study. Because implications usually are presented near the end of a research report, when they are included in an abstract, they usually should be at the end of the abstract.

Example 11.5.A [8]

Five hundred and five respondents, from a wide variety of business organizations, were surveyed to gather information on their perceptions of nonverbal communication. Dividing the sample on the basis of perceived decoding ability and gender revealed several differences between the groups. Nonverbal communication was more important to self-rated good decoders than to other decoders. Better decoders relied most on facial expressions. . . .

Recommendations for improved communication in businesses included paying more attention to nonverbal cues, especially to facial expressions, engaging in more eye contact, and probing for more information when verbal and nonverbal cues are discrepant. Managers should be aware that most employees feel frustrations and distrust when receiving conflicting signals from their supervisors, and should try to modify their behavior by being more honest when communicating their emotions.

---

[8] Graham, Unruh, & Jennings (1991, p. 45)

Concluding Comments

Although the abstract is usually the last element of a report to be written, it should not be prepared as a casual afterthought. Rather, it should be planned carefully and structured so that essential highlights are presented in a very limited number of words. A poorly written abstract may lead many potential readers to skip the rest of your report; a well-crafted one, on the other hand, is likely to increase the number of people who choose to read a report of your work.

Exercise for Chapter 11

1. Locate two abstracts for journal articles of interest to you. For each, identify the elements included (i.e., hypotheses or purposes, methodology, analysis and results, significance of the topic, and implications). Read the article and then comment on the adequacy of the abstract.

2. Locate a journal article, thesis, or dissertation of interest to you and read the article without reading the abstract. Write your own abstract for the article and compare it with the abstract prepared by the author of the article. What are the similarities? What are the differences?

3. Examine abstracts in *Dissertation Abstracts International*, which is available in most academic libraries. Locate one that you think is well written and that covers, in order, these points:

(a) research purposes of hypotheses, (b) methodology, and (c) results. Copy the abstract and bring it to class for discussion.

Notes:

References

Baratta, J. E., & McManus, M. A. (1992). The effect of contextual factors on individuals' job performance. *Journal of Applied Social Psychology, 22,* 1702–1710.

Beattie, V. & Jones, M. J. (1992). The use and abuse of graphs in annual reports: Theoretical framework and empirical study. *Accounting and Business Research, 22,* 291–303.

Bemmaor, A. C., & Mouchoux, D. (1991). Measuring the short-term effect of in-store promotion and retail advertising on brand sales: A factorial experiment. *Journal of Marketing Research, XXVIII,* 202–214.

Boeker, W. (1992). Power and managerial dismissal: Scapegoating at the top. *Administrative Science Quarterly, 37,* 400–421.

Bozeman, B., Reed, P. N., & Scott, P. (1992). Red tape and task delays in public and private organizations. *Administration and Society, 24,* 290–322.

Brockner, J., Tyler, T. R., & Cooper-Schneider, R. (1992). The influence of prior commitment to an institution on reactions to perceived unfairness: The higher they are, the harder they fall. *Administrative Science Quarterly, 37,* 241–261.

Brownell, J. (1990). Perceptions of effective listeners: A management study. *Journal of Business Communication, 27,* 401–415.

Bucklin, R. E., & Srinivasan, V. (1991). Determining interbrand substitutability through survey measurement of consumer preference structures. *Journal of Marketing Research, XXVIII,* 58–71.

Burns, L.D., & Caughey, C. C. (1992). Category use in first impressions of restaurant interiors. *Perceptual and Motor Skills, 75,* 107–110.

Chamblee, R., & Sandler, D. M. (1992). Business-to-business advertising: Which layout style works best? *Journal of Advertising Research, 32,* 39–46.

Chang, H. (1991). The effects of a decision support system on novice personnel managers in their evaluation of candidates applying for programmer/analyst positions. *Dissertation Abstracts International, 53,* 214A. (Order number DA92 16905)

References

Chao, G. T., Walz, P. M., & Gardner, P. D. (1992). Formal and informal mentorships: A comparison on mentoring functions and contrast with nonmentored counterparts. *Personnel Psychology, 45*, 619–627.

Clampitt, P. G., & Downs, C. W. (1993). Employee perceptions of the relationship between communication and productivity: A field study. *The Journal of Business Communication, 30*, 5–28.

Coughlan, A. T., & Narasimhan, C. (1992). An empirical analysis of sales-force compensation plans. *Journal of Business, 65*, 93–121.

Cox, A. D., & Cox, D. (1990). Competing on price: The role of retail price advertisements in shaping store-price image. *Journal of Retailing, 66*, 428–445.

Cox, T. H., & Harquail, C. V. (1991). Career paths and career success in the early career stages of male and female MBA's. *Journal of Vocational Behavior, 39*, 54–75.

Davy, J. A., & Shipper, F. (1993). Voter behavior in union certification elections: A longitudinal study. *Academy of Management Journal, 36*, 187–199.

Dawson, S., Bloch, P. H., & Ridgway, N. M. (1990). Shopping motives, emotional states, and retail outcomes. *Journal of Retailing, 66*, 408–427.

Dion, P. A., & Notarantonio, E. M. (1992). Salesperson communication style: The neglected dimension in sales performance. *Journal of Business Communication, 29*, 63–77.

Gatewood, R., Lahiff, J., Deter, R., & Hargrove, L. (1989). Effects of training on behaviors of the selections interview. *Journal of Business Communication, 26*, 17–31.

Gotlieb, J. B., & Dubinsky, A. J. (1991). Influence of price on aspects of consumers' cognitive process. *Journal of Applied Psychology, 76*, 541–549.

Ginsberg, A., & Abrahamson, E. (1991). Champions of change and strategic shifts: The role of internal and external change advocates. *Journal of Management Studies, 28*, 173–190.

Graham, G. H., Unruh, J., & Jennings, P. (1991). The impact of nonverbal communication in organizations: A survey of perceptions. *The Journal of Business Communication, 28*, 45–62.

Graves, L. M., & Karren, R. J. (1992). Interviewer decision processes and effectiveness: An experimental policy-capturing investigation. *Personnel Psychology, 45*, 313–340.

Greller, M. M. (1992). Feedback on job performance and expected career advancement. *Perceptual and Motor Skills, 75*, 1323–1329.

Gulbro, R. D. (1991). Human Resource Management practices in successful small manufacturing companies. *Dissertation Abstracts International, 53*, 216A–217A. (Order number DA9218191).

152

Gupta, S., & Cooper, L. G. (1992). The discounting of discounts and promotion thresholds. *Journal of Consumer Research, 19*, 401–411.

Harrell, W. A., & Reid, E. E. (1990). Safety of children in grocery stores: The impact of carseat use in shopping carts and parental monitoring. *Accident Analysis and Prevention, 22*, 531–542.

Hennart, J. (1991). The transaction costs theory of joint ventures: An empirical study of Japanese subsidiaries in the United States. *Management Science, 37*, 483–497.

Higgins, C. A., Duxbury, L. E., & Irving, R. H. (1992). Work-family conflict in the dual career family. *Organizational Behavior and Human Decision Processes, 51*, 51–75.

Hornik, J., & Ellis, S. (1988). Strategies to secure compliance for a mall intercept interview. *Public Opinion Quarterly, 52*, 539–551.

Ibarra, H. (1992). Homophily and differential returns: Sex differences in network structure and access in an advertising firm. *Administrative Science Quarterly, 37*, 422–447.

Igbaria, M., & Greenhaus, J. H. (1992). The career advancement prospects of managers and professionals: Are MIS employees unique? *Decision Sciences Journal, 23*, 478–499.

Jaffe, L. J., Jamieson, L. F., & Berger, P. D. (1992). Impact of comprehension, positioning, and segmentation on advertising response. *Journal of Advertising Research, 32*, 24–33.

Kalwani, M. U., & Yim, C. K. (1992). Consumer price and promotion expectations: An experimental study. *Journal of Marketing Research, 29*, 90–100

Klaas, B. S., Heneman, H. G., & Olson, C. A. (1991). Effects of grievance activity on absenteeism. *Journal of Applied Psychology, 76*, 818–824.

Libby, R., & Lipe, M. G. (1992). Incentives, effort, and the cognitive processes involved in accounting-related judgments. *Journal of Accounting Research, 30*, 249–273.

Lyne, S. R. (1992). Perceptions and attitudes of different user-groups to the role of the budget, budget pressure, and budget participation. *Accounting and Business Research, 22*, 357–369.

McDonald, L. M., & Korabik, K. (1991). Sources of stress and ways of coping among male and female managers. *Journal of Social Behavior and Personality, 6*, 185–198.

Melcher, D., Eichstedt, J. L., Eriksen, S., & Clawson, D. (1992). Women's participation in local union leadership: The Massachusetts experience. *Industrial and Labor Relations Review, 45*, 267–280.

Morrison, R. F., & Brantner, T. M. (1992). What enhances or inhibits learning a new job? A basic issue. *Journal of Applied Psychology, 77*, 926–940.

Morwitz, V. G., & Schmittlein, D. (1992). Using segmentation to improve sales forecasts based on purchase intent: Which "intenders" actually buy? *Journal of Marketing Research, XXIX*, 391–405.

Muehling, D. D., Stem, D. E., & Raven, P. (1989). Comparative advertising: Views from advertisers, agencies, media, and policy makers. *Journal of Advertising Research, 29*, 38–48.

Narus, J. A., & Guimaraes, T. (1987). Computer usage in distributor marketing. *Industrial Marketing Management, 16*, 43–54.

Newell, S. (1992). The myth and destructiveness of equal opportunities: The continued dominance of the mothering role. *Personnel Review, 21*, 37–47.

Ostroff, C., & Kozlowski, S. W. (1992). Organizational socialization as a learning process: The role of information acquisition. *Personnel Psychology, 45*, 849–874.

Poole, M. E., Langan-Fox, J., & Omodei, M. (1991). Career orientations in women from rural and urban backgrounds. *Human Relations, 44*, 9883–1005.

Powell, G. N. (1991). Applicant reactions to the initial employment interview: Exploring theoretical and methodological issues. *Personnel Psychology, 44*, 67–83.

Prakash, V. (1992). Sex roles and advertising preferences. *Journal of Advertising Research, 32*, 43–52.

Raimondo, H. J., Esposito, L., & Gershenberg, I. (1990). Introductory class size and student performance in intermediate theory courses. *Journal of Economic Education, 21*, 369–381.

Ralston, D. A., Gustafson, D. J., Elsass, P. M., Cheung, F., & Terpstra, R. H. (1992). Eastern values: A comparison of managers in the United States, Hong Kong, and the People's Republic of China. *Journal of Applied Psychology, 77*, 664–671.

Reitsperger, W. D., & Daniel, S. J. (1991). A comparison of quality attitudes in the USA and Japan: Empirical evidence. *Journal of Management Studies, 28*, 585–599.

Rao, A. R., & Bergen, M. E. (1992). Price premium variations as a consequence of buyers' lack of information. *Journal of Consumer Research, 19*, 412–423.

Rao, A. R., & Sieben, W. A. (1992). The effect of prior knowledge on price acceptability and the type of information examined. *Journal of Consumer Research, 19*, 256–270.

Rasch, R. H., & Tosi, H. L. (1992). Factors affecting software developers' performance: An integrated approach. *MIS Quarterly, 16*, 395–409.

Reider, M. (1987). *The validity of telephone reports in clinical follow-ups: Follow-ups of former participants in a weight reduction program*. Unpublished master's thesis, California State University, Los Angeles.

Sawyer, A. G., & Howard, D. J. (1991). Effects of omitting conclusions in advertisements to involved and uninvolved audiences. *Journal of Marketing Research, XXVIII*, 467–474.

Schermerhorn, J. R., Jr., Gardner, W. L. III, & Dresdow, S. A. (1992). *Journal of Management Education, 16*, 430–443.

Schilit, W. K. (1990). A comparative analysis of strategic decisions. *Journal of Management Studies, 27*, 435–461.

Schwarzwald, J., Koslowsky, M., & Shalit, B. (1992). A field study of employee's attitudes and behaviors after promotion decisions. *Journal of Applied Psychology, 77*, 511-514.

Sheffey, S., & Tindale, R. S. (1992). Perceptions of sexual harassment in the workplace. *Journal of Applied Social Psychology, 22*, 1502–1520.

Singh, S. N., & Cole, C. A. (1993). The effects of length, content, and repetition on television commercial effectiveness. *Journal of Marketing Research, XXX*, 91–104.

Stopford, J. M., & Baden-Fuller, C. (1990). Corporate rejuvenation. *Journal of Management Studies, 27*, 399–415.

Stroh, L. K., Brett, J. M., & Reilly, A. H. (1992). All the right stuff: A comparison of female and male managers. *Journal of Applied Psychology, 77*, 251–260.

Tilly, C. (1992). Dualism in part-time employment. *Industrial Relations, 31*, 330–347.

Torkzadeh, G., & Xia, W. (1992). Managing telecommunications by steering committee. *MIS Quarterly, 16*, 187–199.

Trevino, L. K., & Victor, B. (1992). Peer reporting of unethical behavior: A social context perspective. *Academy of Management Journal, 35*, 38–64.

Unnava, H. R., & Burnkrant, R. E. (1991). Effects of repeating varied ad executions on brand name memory. *Journal of Marketing Research, XXVIII*, 406–416.

Usunier, J. C. G. (1991). Business time perceptions and national cultures: A comparative survey. *Management International Review, 31*, 197–209.

Vance, C. M., McClaine, S. R., Boje, D. M., & Stage, H. D. (1992). An examination of the transferability of traditional performance appraisal principles across cultural boundaries. *Management International Review, 32*, 313–326.

Wansink, B., & Ray, M. L. (1992). Estimating an advertisement's impact on one's consumption of a brand. *Journal of Advertising Research, 32*, 9–16.

Wheeler, S., & Lyon, D. (1992). Employee benefits for the employer's benefit: How companies respond to Employee Stress. *Personnel Review, 21*, 47–65.

Widing, R. E., Hoverstad, R., Coulter, R., & Brown, G. (1991). The VASE scales: Measures of viewpoints about sexual embeds in advertising. *Journal of Business Research, 22*, 3–10.

Witt, L. A., & Nye, L. G. (1992). Gender and the relationship between perceived fairness of pay or promotion and job satisfaction. *Journal of Applied Psychology, 77,* 910–917.

Zenger, T. R. (1992). Why do employers only reward extreme performance? Examining the relationships among performance, pay, and turnover. *Administrative Science Quarterly, 37,* 198–219.

Zimmer, M. R., & Golden, L. L. (1988). Impressions of retail stores: A content analysis of consumer images. *Journal of Retailing, 64,* 265–293.

Appendix A

Checklist of Guidelines

Chapter 1   Writing Simple Research Hypotheses

_____ 1.1 A simple research hypothesis should name two variables and indicate the type of relationship expected between them.

_____ 1.2 When a relationship is expected only among a certain type of subject, the population should be mentioned in the hypothesis.

_____ 1.3 A simple hypothesis should be as specific as possible yet expressed in a single sentence.

_____ 1.4 If a comparison is to be made, the elements to be compared should be stated.

_____ 1.5 Because most hypotheses deal with the behavior of groups, plural forms should usually be used.

_____ 1.6 A hypothesis should be free of terms and phrases that do not add to its meaning.

_____ 1.7 A hypothesis should indicate what will actually be studied—not the possible implications of the study or value judgments of the author.

_____ 1.8 A hypothesis usually should name variables in the order in which they occur or will be measured.

_____ 1.9 Avoid using the words "significant" or "significance" in a hypothesis.

_____ 1.10 Avoid using the word "prove" in a hypothesis.

_____ 1.11 Avoid using more than one term to refer to a given variable.

Chapter 2   A Closer Look at Hypotheses

_____ 2.1 A "statement of the hypotheses" may contain more than one hypothesis. It is permissible to include them in a single sentence as long as the sentence is reasonably concise and its meaning is clear.

_____ 2.2 When a number of related hypotheses are to be stated, consider presenting them in a numbered or lettered list.

_____ 2.3 The hypothesis or hypotheses should be placed before the section on methods.

_____ 2.4 It is permissible, but *not* recommended, to use terms other than *hypothesis* to refer to a hypothesis.

_____ 2.5 A hypothesis may be stated without indicating the type of relationship expected between variables, but to qualify as a hypothesis, it must specify that some unknown type of relationship is expected.

_____ 2.6 When a researcher has a research hypothesis, it should be stated in the research paper; the null hypothesis does not always need to be stated.

_____ 2.7 Avoid using the word "significant" in the statement of the null hypothesis.

Chapter 3 Writing Research Purposes, Objectives, and Questions

_____ 3.1 When there are many hypotheses, consider providing a general statement of purpose before stating the specific hypotheses.

_____ 3.2 When the goal of research is to describe variables without describing relationships among them, state a research purpose or question instead of a hypothesis.

_____ 3.3 Research purposes or questions should be stated when not enough is known to permit formulation of hypotheses.

_____ 3.4 A research purpose or question should be as specific as possible, yet stated concisely.

_____ 3.5 When a number of related purposes or questions are to be stated, the author should consider presenting them in a numbered or lettered list.

Chapter 4 Writing Titles

_____ 4.1 If only a small number of variables are studied, the title should name the variables.

_____ 4.2 If many variables are studied, only the types of variables should be named.

_____ 4.3 The title of a journal article should be concise; the title of a thesis or dissertation may be longer.

_____ 4.4 A title should indicate what was studied—not the results of the study.

_____ 4.5 Mention the population(s) in a title when the type(s) of population(s) are important.

_____ 4.6 Consider the use of subtitles to indicate the methods of study or amplify the variable(s) mentioned in the main title.

_____ 4.7 A title may be stated in the form of a question; this form should be used sparingly and with caution.

_____ 4.8 Use the words "effect" and "influence" in titles with caution.

_____ 4.9 A title should be consistent with the research hypothesis, purpose, or question.

_____ 4.10 Avoid clever titles, especially if they fail to communicate important information about the report.

_____ 4.11 Use brand names in titles sparingly.

Chapter 5 Writing Introductions and Literature Reviews

_____ 5.1 Consider starting the introduction by describing the problem area and gradually shift its focus to specific research hypotheses, purposes, or questions.

_____ 5.2 In long introductions and literature reviews, consider the use of subheadings to guide readers.

_____ 5.3 The significance of a topic should be explicitly stated in the introduction to a term paper, thesis, or dissertation.

_____ 5.4 A statement of significance should be specific to the topic investigated.

_____ 5.5 Use of the first person is acceptable; it should be used when it facilitates the smooth flow of the introduction, but it should be used sparingly.

_____ 5.6 The literature review should be presented in the form of an essay—not in the form of an annotated list.

_____ 5.7 The literature review should emphasize the findings of previous research—not just the methodologies and variables studied.

_____ 5.8 Point out trends and themes in the literature.

_____ 5.9 Point out gaps in the literature.

_____ 5.10 Use the literature review to establish the need for the current study.

_____ 5.11 The author should feel free to express opinions about the quality and importance of the research being cited.

_____ 5.12 The literature review for a journal article should be highly selective; the review for a thesis or dissertation may be less selective.

_____ 5.13 Consider citing older literature in order to provide a historical context for the present study.

_____ 5.14 Use direct quotations sparingly in literature reviews.

_____ 5.15 Report sparingly the details of the literature being cited.

Chapter 6 Writing Definitions

_____ 6.1 All of the variables in a research hypothesis, purpose, or question should be defined.

_____ 6.2 Most abbreviations should be defined the first time they are used.

_____ 6.3 Theories and models on which a thesis or dissertation are based should be formally defined. In a journal article, the author may choose to provide an informal definition and refer the reader to a publication in which it is described in detail if the theory is well-known in the author's field.

_____ 6.4 Conceptual definitions should be specific.

_____ 6.5 Operational definitions should be provided. As noted above, these are usually stated in the method section of a report or proposal.

_____ 6.6 If a published instrument was used, the variable measured by that instrument may be operationally defined by citing the reference for it.

_____ 6.7 If an unpublished instrument was used, the whole instrument should be reproduced in the report or a source for a copy of the instrument should be provided in order to define operationally the variable that was measured.

_____ 6.8 Operational definitions should be sufficiently specific so that another investigator can replicate a study with confidence that he or she is examining the same variables under the same circumstances.

_____ 6.9 Even a highly operational definition may not be a useful definition.

Chapter 7 Writing Assumptions and Limitations

_____ 7.1 In the statement of an assumption, consider stating the reason(s) why it was necessary to make the assumption.

_____ 7.2 If there is a reason for believing an assumption is true, state the reason.

_____ 7.3 If an assumption is highly questionable, consider casting it as a limitation.

_____ 7.4 Consider speculating on the possible effects of a limitation on the results of the study.

_____ 7.5 When space permits, be specific in a statement of limitations.

Chapter 8 Writing Method Sections

_____ 8.1 The subjects should be described in enough detail so that the reader can visualize the subjects.

_____ 8.2 A population should be named and the method used to select the sample should be described.

_____ 8.3 If there was attrition, state the number of subjects who dropped out, the reasons for the attrition, if known, and information about the dropouts, if available.

_____ 8.4 If an unpublished instrument was used, describe it in detail.

_____ 8.5 If a published instrument was used, briefly describe the traits that it was designed to measure, its format, scoring procedures, and the possible range of score values.

_____ 8.6 In theses and dissertations, information on reliability and validity should be described in detail; in journal articles, a brief summary of information on reliability and validity is usually sufficient, and it may be sufficient only to refer to a published source of information on these topics if the instrument is well known and in widespread use.

_____ 8.7 Physical procedures, equipment, and other mechanical matters should be described in sufficient detail so that the study can be replicated.

Chapter 9 Writing Analysis and Results Sections

_____ 9.1 Organize the analysis and results section around the research hypotheses (or purposes or questions) stated in the introduction; describe the analysis and results for the first hypothesis first, then describe them for the second hypothesis, and so on.

_____ 9.2 Standard statistical procedures need only be named; you do not need to show the formulas.

_____ 9.3 Raw scores are usually not reported; only the statistics based on them are reported.

_____ 9.4 Present descriptive statistics first, usually starting with measures of central tendency and variability (or, for categorical data, starting with frequencies and percentages).

_____ 9.5 Organize large amounts of data in tables and give each table a number and a descriptive title (i.e., caption).

_____ 9.6 In the text, describe the main conclusions to be reached based on each table and point out highlights that the reader may otherwise overlook. You do not need to discuss each entry in a table.

_____ 9.7 Statistical figures (i.e., drawings such as pie charts and bar graphs) should be professionally drawn and used sparingly in journal articles.

_____ 9.8 All tables and figures in a report should be referred to in the body of the text.

_____ 9.9 Statistical symbols should be underlined or italicized.

_____ 9.10 Use the proper case for each statistical symbol.

_____ 9.11 Numerals that start sentences and that are less than 12 usually should be spelled out.

_____ 9.12 The term *significance* often should be modified with an adjective—either *statistical* or *practical.*

_____ 9.13 Qualitative results need to be organized and the organization made clear to the reader.

Chapter 10   Writing Discussion Sections

_____ 10.1 A brief summary of the study may be included in the discussion section of a journal article; a long, detailed summary may be required in a thesis or dissertation.

_____ 10.2 Consider beginning the discussion section with a restatement of the research purposes, questions, or hypotheses.

_____ 10.3 Explicitly state whether the research hypotheses were supported. If research questions were stated instead of hypotheses, explicitly answer the questions.

_____ 10.4 Highlights of the results should be described in the discussion section.

_____ 10.5 Explicitly state the implications of the results in the discussion section.

_____ 10.6 Important strengths and limitations should be mentioned in the discussion section.

_____ 10.7 If you issue a call for further research on a problem, provide the reader with specific guidance.

_____ 10.8 Point out consistencies and inconsistencies of the current results with those in the literature cited earlier in the report.

_____ 10.9 It is acceptable to speculate on the meaning of the results.

_____ 10.10 It is usually inappropriate to introduce new data or new references to literature in the discussion and conclusion section.

_____ 10.11 Provide subheadings within long discussion sections.

Chapter 11 Writing Abstracts

_____ 11.1 Highlights of the results usually should be included in an abstract.

_____ 11.2 Highlights of the methodology usually should be mentioned, especially if the methodology is superior to that used in previous studies.

_____ 11.3 Reference to the research hypotheses or purposes may be made.

_____ 11.4 It is sometimes appropriate to point out the significance of the topic in abstract.

_____ 11.5 It is sometimes appropriate to summarize the implications of the results.

Notes:

Appendix B

Style Guide for Authors: Articles
Academy of Management Journal[1]

Submit five copies of the manuscript; be sure that they are good, clear copies and that all pages are included in each copy. The manuscript should by typed on standard size (8½" x 11") paper, *double-spaced throughout* (including footnotes, references, quotations, and appendixes), on only one side of the paper, and with wide margins (one inch or more) at top, bottom, and both sides of each page. Manuscripts prepared on computers should be printed on letter-quality printers or, if other printers are used, in double-strike or enhanced print. Footnotes, references, appendixes, tables, and figures should be on separate sheets of paper and should be arranged at the end of the manuscript in the order listed in this sentence. There is no absolute limit, but the length of articles should not ordinarily exceed 30 manuscript pages, including references, appendixes, tables, and figures.

Title Page and Abstract

The first page of the manuscript should include the title of the article (typed in all capital letters), the authors' names (typed in all capitals), and their affiliations, addresses, and phone numbers (typed with initial caps only). Example:

THE EFFECTS OF AN ACQUISITIVE GROWTH STRATEGY ON FIRM PERFORMANCE

MICHAEL A. HITT

College of Business Administration

Texas A&M University

College Station, TX 77843-4221

(409) 845-1724

No mention of authors' names should be made in the body of the paper, except where appropriate in citations and references.

The second page, numbered page 2, should repeat the title and include an abstract of 75 words or less. The text of the article should begin on page 3. Page numbering should continue through all pages of the manuscript, including those with footnotes, references, appendixes, tables, and figures.

Acknowledgments

An unnumbered footnote can be used to acknowledge financial support and/or assistance of others in preparing the manuscript. In the manuscript, the text for this footnote should appear at the bottom of the same page as the abstract (page 2). It should be separated from the abstract by a 10-dash line beginning at the left-hand margin.

Footnotes

Other footnotes should be used sparingly. Minimize their use for parenthetical discussion; material that is pertinent can often be integrated into the text. They should *not* be used for citing references (see References below). The text for all footnotes should appear on a separate page or pages at the end of the body of the article.

Headings

Main headings should be used to designate the major sections of the article; three or four main headings should be sufficient for most articles. Initial headings, such as "Introduction," are unnecessary. Main headings should be centered on the page and typed in all capitals. They should not be underlined. Example:

METHODS

Secondary headings should be typed flush with the left margin and in small letters, with major words beginning with capitals. Secondary headings should not be underlined. Example:

Sample

Third-order or *paragraph headings* should begin with a standard paragraph indention and be typed in capital and small letters, with only the initial word capitalized. Paragraph headings should be followed by a period; they should not be underlined. Example:

Manager sample. Respondents consisted of a random sample of 300 managers. . . .

The text should follow on the same line.

Tables and Figures

Useful tables and figures do not duplicate the text; they supplement and clarify it. Because tables and figures are considerably more expensive to prepare for publication than text, the degree to which they add to the impact of the manuscript should be considered carefully.

Tables should be typed, double-spaced, on separate pages (one page for each table) from the text. They should be grouped together following the appendixes. If there is no appendix, tables should follow the references. For most papers, the first table should report descriptive statistics, including means, standard deviations, and a complete intercorrelation matrix. Each table should have the word TABLE (typed in all caps) and its number (arabic numerals) centered at the top. The table title should be in capital and small letters and centered on the page directly under the table number; it should not be underlined. Example:

TABLE 1

Firms in Sample

Tables should be numbered consecutively from the beginning to the end of the article. The position of the table in the manuscript should be indicated in the text as follows:

Insert Table 1 about here

Footnotes to tables are of two types:

(1) General footnotes that explain the table as a whole, the designations of table columns or rows, or an individual item. All of these should be designated by superscript small letters ([a,b,c]), with the footnotes for each separate table beginning with [a].

(2) Footnotes used to indicate the level of significance should follow any other footnotes and be designated by one or more asterisks: * for $p < .05$, ** for $p < .01$, and *** for $p < .001$. Use a dagger symbol (†) for $p < .10$.

If it is necessary to distinguish some numerals in a table from others (for example, to indicate which factor loadings define a factor), boldface type can be used. In the typed manuscript, any numerals that should be set in boldface type should be underlined with a wavy line.

This possibility should not be used when other conventions, such as footnotes, are sufficient.

Figures are any illustrations other than tables. Authors should be prepared to supply finished camera-ready artwork for all figures at the time the manuscript is accepted for publication. Unless the authors are highly skilled in graphics, a professional drafting service should be employed to prepare figures.

The spacing and lettering used in figures should allow for subsequent reduction in size by as much as 50 percent so that the figure will fit the size of the *Journal's* page. The original artwork for figures should not be submitted until after the manuscript has been accepted for publication.

Figures should be numbered consecutively with arabic numerals and their position in the text indicated as for tables (see above). Each figure should be presented on a separate page with FIGURE (typed in all caps) and its number centered above it and a short identifying title in capital and small letters centered underneath the figure number. Example:

FIGURE 1

Model of Contextual Influences on Performance

The position of the figure in the manuscript should be indicated in the text as follows:

Insert Figure 1 about here

References

An alphabetically ordered list of references cited in the text should be included at the end of the article. References should begin on a separate page headed REFERENCES. Continue the pagination.

Entries in the list of *references* should be alphabetized by the last name of the author (first author if more than one) or editor, or by the corporate author (U.S. Census Bureau) or periodical name (*Wall Street Journal*) if there is no indication of individual authors or editors. Several references by an identical author (or group of authors) are ordered by year of publication, with the earliest listed first. Multiple references to works by one author or group of authors with the same year of publication should be differentiated with the addition of small letters (a, b, etc.) after the year. Authors' names are repeated for each entry.

Citations to references should be designated throughout the text by enclosing the authors' names and the year of the reference in parentheses. Example:

Several studies (Adams, 1974; Brown & Hales, 1975, 1980; Collins, 1976a,b) support this conclusion.

Note the use of alphabetical order and an ampersand in citations.

Page numbers must be included in a citation to provide the exact source of a direct quotation. Page numbers follow the date of publication given in parentheses and are separated from it by a colon. Example:

Adams has said that writing a book is "a long and arduous task" (1974: 3).

They should also be used when specific arguments or findings of authors are paraphrased or summarized. As indicated in the example, if the name of the author occurs in the body of the sentence, only the year of publication is cited in parentheses. Otherwise, both name and date appear in parentheses, separated by a comma.

If a work has two authors, always cite both names every time the work is cited in the text. If the work has more than two authors, cite all authors the first time the reference occurs; in subsequent citations of the same work, include only the surname of the first author followed by "et al." (not underlined) and the year. Examples:

Few field studies use random assignment (Franz, Johnson, & Schmidt, 1976).

(first citation)

... even when random assignment is not possible (Franz et al., 1976: 23).

(subsequent citation)

However, for works with six or more authors, use only the surname of the first author followed by et al. whenever the work is cited.

Book entries in the list of references follow this form: Authors' or Editors' Last Names, Initials. Year. Title of book. (Book titles are underlined and typed in lower case letters except for the first word and the first word after a colon.) City Where Published, State or Country (only if necessary to identify the city; use U.S. Postal Service abbreviations for state identification): Name of Publisher. Examples:

Boulding, K. E. 1956. The image. Ann Arbor: University of Michigan Press.

Kahn, R. L., & Boulding, E. (Eds.). 1964. Power and conflict in organizations. Glencoe, IL: Free Press.

Katz, D., & Kahn, R. L. 1978. The social psychology of organizations (2d ed.). New York: John Wiley & Sons.

U.S. Department of Labor Statistics. 1976–1983. Employment and earnings. Washington, DC: U.S. Government Printing Office.

Periodical entries follow this form: Authors' Last Names, Initials. Year. Title of article or paper (in lower case letters except for the first word and the first word after a colon). Name of Periodical, volume number (issue number): page numbers. Examples:

Fry, L. W., & Slocum, J. W., Jr. 1984. Technology, structure, and workgroup effectiveness: A test of a contingency model. <u>Academy of Management Journal</u>, 27: 221–246.

Goggin, W. C. 1974. How the multidimensional structure works at Dow Corning. <u>Harvard Business</u> Review, 55 (1): 54–65.

This issue number should only be included if the periodical's pages are not numbered consecutively throughout the volume, that is, if each issue begins with page 1.

If a periodical article has no author, the name of the periodical should be treated like a corporate author, both in the citation and in the references. For example:

There is fear that Social Security rates may rise <u>(Wall Street Journal</u>, 1984).

<u>Wall Street Journal</u>. 1984. Inflation rate may cause Social Security increase. September 24: 14.

Chapters in books follow this form: Authors' Last Names, Initials. Year. Title of chapter (in lower case except for the first word and first word after a colon). In Editors' Initials and Last Names <u>(Eds.),</u> <u>Title of book:</u> page numbers. City Where Published, State or Country (only if necessary to identify the city): Name of Publisher. Examples:

Berg, N. A. 1973. Corporate role in diversified companies. In B. Taylor & I. MacMillan (Eds.), <u>Business</u> <u>policy: Teaching and research</u>: 298–347. New York: John Wiley & Sons.

Roberts, F. S. 1976. Strategy for the energy crisis: The case of commuter transportation policy. In R. Axelrod (Ed.), <u>Structure of decision</u>: 142–179. Princeton, NJ: Princeton University Press.

Unpublished papers, dissertations, and presented papers should be listed in the references using the following formats:

Duncan, R. G. 1971. <u>Multiple decision-making structures in adapting to environmental uncertainty</u>. Working paper no. 54-71, Northwestern University Graduate School of Management, Evanston, IL

Smith, M. H. 1980. <u>A multidimensional approach to individual differences in empathy</u>. Unpublished doctoral dissertation, University of Texas, Austin.

Wall, J. P. 1983. <u>Work and nonwork correlates of the career plateau</u>. Paper presented at the annual meeting of the Academy of Management, Dallas, TX.

Appendixes

Lengthy but essential methodological details, such as explanations of long lists of measures, should be presented in one or more appendixes at the end of the article. This material should be presented in as condensed a form as possible; full sentences are not necessary. No tables should be included in the appendixes. A single appendix should be titled APPENDIX in all caps. If more than one appendix is needed, they should be titled and ordered alphabetically: APPENDIX A, APPENDIX B, etc.

Biographical Sketches

At the time an article is accepted for publication, a brief biographical sketch of 50 words or less should be submitted for each author. It should include where highest degree was earned, present position, affiliation, and current research interests. For example:

Andrea Barber earned her Ph.D. degree at the University of Wisconsin; she is an associate professor of management and Director of the Management Improvement Center at Famous University, Oxbridge, Ohio. Her current research interests include dual-career families and sociotechnical systems in organizations.

RESEARCH NOTES

Research notes contain brief descriptions of original research. To be considered for the Research Notes section, manuscripts should not exceed 15 double-spaced typewritten pages in length. Descriptive surveys, replications, methodological demonstrations or analyses, studies that make incremental advances to established areas of inquiry, and commentaries with new empirical content are especially appropriate.

Manuscripts intended for the Research Notes section should be prepared according to the above instructions for articles, except that the abstract should not exceed 50 words in length.

GENERAL USAGE

Avoidance of Sexist and Other Biased Language

Authors must avoid terms or usages that are or may be interpreted as denigrating to ethnic or other groups. Authors should be particularly careful in dealing with gender, where long-established customs (e.g., the use of " men and girls" in the office or "usually if the employee is given an opportunity, he will make the right choice") can imply inferiority where none exists or the acceptance of inequality where none should be tolerated. Using plural pronouns (e.g., changing the "client . . . he" to "clients . . . they") is preferred by Academy publications. If this is not possible, the phrase "he or she" can and should be used.

Use of First Person

Vigorous, direct, clear, and concise communication should be the objective of all articles in Academy journals. Although third-person style traditionally has been used, authors can use the first person and active voice if they do not dominate the communication or sacrifice the objectivity of the research.

Appendix C

Manuscript Guidelines
Journal of Retailing[1]

The primary objective of the *Journal of Retailing* is to serve as a medium for new and significant contributions to the theoretical and practical understanding of retailing. The *Journal's* readers represent a variety of academic disciplines as well as the practical domain of retail management. Therefore, authors should include valid generalizations based on their findings that permit the transfer of knowledge from a specific empirical context to a broader level of meaning and relevance.

Each manuscript is reviewed by at least two reviewers knowledgeable in the subject area addressed. Their evaluations are based on the objectives and criteria of the *Journal of Retailing* as well as on established standards of scientific quality. The identity of authors is withheld from reviewers. The decision of the editor concerning publication of a manuscript is influenced considerably by the reviewers' opinions. The decision and the reasons for it are communicated promptly to the authors, usually within 60 days, after receipt of their manuscripts.

Submit four nonreturnable copies of each manuscript to the Editor, *Journal of Retailing*, New York University, 202 Tisch Hall, Washington Square, New York, NY 10003. Manuscripts must be typed double-spaced on 8½ x 11-inch pages with 1-inch margins on all sides.

Title Page. The title of the manuscript, the name, title, affiliation, address, and phone number of each author, the date, and any

---

[1]Reprinted with permission from the *Journal of Retailing*.

acknowledgment of financial or technical assistance should appear on the title page.

Abstract. The title of the manuscript and a 100-word abstract substantively summarizing the article should begin the numbered pages (page 1).

Text. Begin the main text on a new page. A brief orientation to the focus of your study should precede the literature review.

In general, your presentation will be enhanced by a concise style and minimal redundancy from one section to the next. For instance, issues that have been put forth in the literature review or the methodology section should be referred to, if appropriate, in abbreviated form in later sections. Similarly, data presented in a table or figure should not be described in detail in the text; cite only those findings that are of particular relevance to your discussion. See the Executive Summary section, below, regarding the relationship of the Executive Summary to the main text.

Headings and subheadings should be used to help the reader follow the flow of the paper. Primary headings are centered, in upper case. Secondary headings are flush left, in upper and lower case. The first line of each paragraph is indented.

Authors are asked to take special care with their presentation of equations and the capitalization and italicization of algebraic symbols. Spell out the numbers one through twenty in the text; use numerals for larger numbers. Spell out the word "percent" in the text. Where spelling or hyphenation is optional, be consistent throughout the manuscript.

Reference citations within the text should consist of the cited author's last name and the year of publication, enclosed in parentheses and without punctuation, for example: (Hendon 1976). If the author's name appears in the sentence, only the year of publication should appear in parentheses, for example: ". . .as suggested by Markin, Lillis, and Narayana (1976)." References to multiple works should occur within one set of parentheses, separated by semicolons, as in: (Mathis and Jackson 1979; Megginson 1977; Hershey 1971). Whenever possible, references should appear immediately before a punctuation mark.

Reference List. The reference list should begin on a separate page and should be typed double-spaced, with the first line of each entry even with the left margin and subsequent lines indented five spaces. Sort references by the first author's last name: multiple papers by the same authors should be listed in chronological order. Use the examples below as a guide to reference style.

Book: Hall, Margaret, John Knapp, and Christopher Winston (1981). *Distribution in Great Britain and North America,* Oxford, England: Oxford University Press.

Journal article: Cummings, Thomas G., and Susan L. Masering (1977), "The Relationship between Worker Alienation and Work-Related Behavior," *Journal of Vocational Behavior,* **10** (April), 167-179.

Book chapter: Katona, George, and Eva Muller (1963), "A Study of Purchasing Decisions," in *Consumer Behavior: A Study of Purchasing Decisions,* Lincoln H. Clark (ed.), New York: New York University Press, 30-87.

Conference proceedings paper: Westbrook, R. A., and R. L. Oliver (1980), "Developing Better Measures of Consumer Satisfaction: Some Preliminary Results," in *Advances in Consumer Research, IX,* K. B. Monroe (ed.), Ann Arbor, Mich.: Association for Consumer Research.

Unpublished work: Rein, Martin, and S. M. Miller, "The Demonstration Project as a Strategy of Change," paper read at Mobilization for Youth Training Institute Workshop, April 30, 1964, at Columbia University, New York, N.Y. Mimeographed.

If the author(s) are cited in the immediately following entries, a 1-inch line should be substituted for each repeated name.

If two or more works by the same author have the same publication date, they should be differentiated by letters (*a, b, c*) after the date. The letter should also appear with the citation in the text.

Footnotes to Text. Footnotes should be used only for the purpose of extending or closing a point in the text. Footnotes, numbered consecutively throughout the manuscript, should be typed, double-spaced, on a separate page.

Tables and Figures. Each table and each figure should be numbered consecutively in arabic numerals and should appear on a separate page. The title should be in upper and lower case and centered. Authors should be prepared to supply camera-ready, original artwork for all figures when the manuscript is accepted. Footnotes for tables and figures should be indicated by *a, b, c,* and so forth.

Consider whether your data might be more effectively presented in a figure, rather than a table. If a table is used, make it as uncluttered as possible. For instance, it is usually preferable to include either percentages or frequencies, and not both. As mentioned above, it is not necessary to discuss tables or figures exhaustively in the text.

Executive Summary. A two- to three-page executive summary must be included at the end of the manuscript, beginning on a separate page. The first one or two paragraphs should briefly describe the research problem, approach used, and findings. The balance of the executive summary should discuss managerial implications of the methodology, the findings, and/or any potential extensions of this research. The entire summary should be written in nontechnical language. Aside from the introductory paragraphs, redundancy with the main text of the paper should be minimized. All discussion of managerial implications should be presented in the executive summary, not in the body of the text.

Appendix D

Guidelines for Authors
The Journal of Management Studies[1]

The Journal of Management Studies aims to publish papers that advance knowledge and address practice in the areas of organization theory, strategic management and human resource management.

By 'advance knowledge' we mean that papers should aim to develop empirically grounded theory that increases our understanding of behaviour in and of organizations in their environments. We recognize that this very statement may be viewed as problematic. Different authors will conceptualize 'behaviour', 'organizations', 'environments', as well as 'in' and 'of' in different ways according to their different theoretical positions. Accordingly we would emphasize that we welcome contributions from a whole gamut of perspectives. Our only proviso is that each author should seek to maintain congruity within his or her own ontological, epistemological and methodological positions in the conduct and reporting of research. Our ultimate criterion for a paper's acceptability is that an informed reader is likely to learn something new from it that contributes to the development of coherent bodies of knowledge.

By 'address practice' we mean that papers should enable practitioners or those who teach practitioners, to gain insight into issues of strategic choice, organizational design and employee relations in their broadest senses. While prescriptive papers are welcome, these must be

---

[1] Reprinted with permission from *The Journal of Management Studies*.

grounded in research and experience, with reasoned justification for the prescriptions advocated.

We welcome papers of between 5000–7000 words. In our experience papers shorter than 5000 words tend to verge either on the slight (and in need of development) or on the trivial (and hence unpublishable). Papers longer than 7000 words at best may contain several embryonic papers worthy of separate development or, at worst, to be unfocused, wordy and repetitious. The editors place great emphasis on clear written style expressing a well structured presentation of ideas.

Manuscript Preparation

Manuscripts of articles from intending contributors should be sent direct to the General Editors. They should be typewritten on one side of the paper only, double spaced, with generous margins, and they should not normally exceed 7000 words. Three copies are requested. Each copy should be accompanied by a separate 200 word abstract summarizing the main argument of the paper.

To permit anonymity of refereeing the author(s) name should not appear on the manuscript proper. Instead, attach a cover page giving the title of the article and the name and affiliation of each author. The title of the manuscript should additionally appear on the first page of the text.

Where authors' names appear in the text, dates and appropriate page references should be supplied and the following conventions observed: Where an author's name appears, the date should follow, in brackets, e.g., Mintzberg (1985). Where references are made to specific pages or a quotation is used, the author's name, date and page references should appear, e.g., Mintzberg (1985, p. 133), if the author's name is present in the text, or, if not (Mintzberg, 1985, p. 133). Where reference is made to more than one author, their names should be in alphabetical order. Appendices where necessary should be placed at the immediate end of the paper. Footnotes, headed 'Notes' and kept to a minimum, should be placed after Appendices, or at the immediate end of the paper if there are no appendices. References to books and articles headed 'References' should be placed in alphabetical order at the end of the paper, directly following the 'Notes' (if any), and the following conventions must be observed:

e.g., *for books*

Morgan, G. (1986). *Images of Organization.* Beverly Hills: Sage.

e.g., *for articles or chapters in edited books*

Pettigrew, A. M. (1987). 'Context and action in the transformation of the firm'. *Journal of Management Studies,* **24,** 6, 649–70.

Kimberly, J. R., Norling, F. and Weiss, J. A. (1983). 'Pondering the performance puzzle'. In Hall, R. H. and Quinn, R. E. (Eds.), *Organizational Theory and Public Policy.* Beverly Hills: Sage, 249-64.

Where a recent edition of a book is referred to, the date of its first publication must also be given.

The editors urge that, particularly in cases where manuscript revision is required, authors double check that books and articles cited in the 'References' actually appear in the text, and vice versa.

The Editors emphasize that manuscripts which do not conform to this format, if accepted, are subject to considerable delay pending copy-editing revisions, since it is not possible to have them typeset until suitable copy has been provided.

Notes:

Appendix E

Instructions to Authors
Journal of Applied Psychology[1]

Articles submitted for publication in the *Journal of Applied Psychology* are evaluated according to the following criteria: (a) significance of contribution, (b) technical adequacy, (c) appropriateness for the journal, and (d) clarity of presentation. In addition, articles must be clearly written in concise and unambiguous language. They must be logically organized, progressing from a statement of problem or purpose, through analysis of evidence, to conclusions and implications.

Authors should prepare manuscripts according to the *Publication Manual of the American Psychological Association* (3rd ed.). Articles not prepared according to the guidelines of the *Manual* will not be reviewed. All manuscripts must include an abstract containing a maximum of 960 characters and spaces (which is approximately 120 words) typed on a separate sheet of paper. Typing instructions (all copy must be double-spaced) and instructions on preparing tables, figures, references, metrics, and abstracts appear in the *Manual*. Also, all manuscripts are subject to editing for sexist language.

Authors can refer to recent issues of the journal for approximate length of regular articles. (Four double-spaced manuscript pages equal one printed page.) A few longer articles of special significance are occasionally published as monographs. Short Notes feature brief reports on studies such as those involving some methodological contribution or important replication. For short notes, length limits are exact and must be strictly followed. In preparing your manuscript, set the character and space limit at 60 characters per line and do not exceed 410 lines for text plus references. These limits do not include the title page, abstract, author note footnotes, tables, or figures. For short notes, as for regular manuscripts, do not exceed 960 characters and spaces in the abstract.

APA policy prohibits an author from submitting the same manuscript for concurrent consideration by two or more publications. In addition, it is a violation of APA Ethical Principles to publish "as original data, data that have been previously published" (Standard 6.24). As this journal is a primary journal that publishes original material only, APA policy prohibits as well publication of any manuscript that has already been published in whole or substantial part elsewhere. Authors have an obligation to consult journal editors concerning prior publication of any data upon which their article depends. In addition, APA Ethical Principles specify that "after research results are published, psychologists do not withhold the data on which their conclusions are based from other competent professionals who seek to verify the substantive claims through reanalysis and who intend to use such data only for that purpose, provided that the confidentiality of the participants can be protected and unless legal rights concerning proprietary data preclude their release" (Standard 6.25). APA expects authors submitting to this journal to adhere to these standards. Specifically, authors of manuscripts submitted to APA journals are expected to have available their data throughout the editorial review process and for at least 5 years after the date of publication.

Authors will be required to state in writing that they have complied with APA ethical standards in the treatment of their sample, human or animal, or to describe the details of treatment. A copy of the APA Ethical Principles may be obtained by writing the APA Ethics Office, 750 First Street, NE, Washington, DC 20002-4242.

Masked reviews are optional, and authors who wish masked reviews must specifically request them when submitting their manuscripts. Each copy of a manuscript to be mask reviewed should include a separate title page with authors' names and affiliations, and these should not appear anywhere else on the manuscript. Footnotes that identify the authors should be typed on a separate page. Authors should make every effort to see that the manuscript itself contains no clues to their identities.

Manuscripts should be submitted in quadruplicate and all the copies should be clear, readable, and on paper of good quality. A dot matrix or unusual typeface is acceptable only if it is clear and legible. In addition to addresses and phone numbers, authors should supply electronic mail addresses and fax numbers, if available, for potential use by the editorial office and later by the production office. Authors should keep a copy of the manuscript to guard against loss. Mail manuscripts to the Editor, Neal Schmitt, Department of Psychology, Michigan State University, East Lansing, Michigan 48824-1117.

Notes:

Form for Evaluating Research Reports[1]

Directions: Read a journal article, thesis, or dissertation assigned to you by your instructor and rate each of the following components on a scale from 5 (very effective) to 1 (very ineffective). Briefly explain your ratings. Keep in mind that a component may be highly effective even if some of the relevant guidelines have been violated.[2]

1. Research Hypotheses, Purposes, Objectives, and Questions (See Chapters 1 through 3.)

    Rating: 5   4   3   2   1

    Explanation:

    _____
    _____
    _____
    _____
    _____
    _____
    _____
    _____
    _____

---

[1]This Appendix may be reproduced in whole or in part without permission by students who have purchased this book or by their instructors.

[2]Review the section on Cautions in Using this Book in the Introduction.

2. Title (See Chapter 4.)

   Rating: 5   4   3   2   1

   Explanation:

   _____
   _____
   _____
   _____
   _____
   _____
   _____
   _____
   _____

3. Introduction and Literature Review (See Chapter 5.)

   Rating: 5   4   3   2   1

   Explanation:

   _____
   _____
   _____
   _____
   _____
   _____
   _____
   _____
   _____

4. Definitions (See Chapter 6.)

Rating: 5   4   3   2   1

Explanation:

_____

_____

_____

_____

_____

_____

_____

_____

_____

5. Assumptions and Limitations (See Chapter 7.)

Rating: 5   4   3   2   1

Explanation:

_____

_____

_____

_____

_____

_____

_____

_____

_____

6. Method (See Chapter 8.)

    Rating: 5   4   3   2   1

    Explanation:

    _____

    _____

    _____

    _____

    _____

    _____

    _____

    _____

    _____

7. Analysis and Results (See Chapter 9.)

    Rating: 5   4   3   2   1

    Explanation:

    _____

    _____

    _____

    _____

    _____

    _____

    _____

    _____

8. Discussion (See Chapter 10.)

Rating: 5   4   3   2   1

Explanation:

_____

_____

_____

_____

_____

_____

_____

_____

9. Abstract (See Chapter 11.)

Rating: 5   4   3   2   1

Explanation:

_____

_____

_____

_____

_____

_____

_____

_____